OCR Philosophy of Religion Revision Guide

H573/1 (Complete Two-Year Course)

By Andrew Capone

Published by Active Education

www.peped.org

First published: 2018
This edition: 2020

ISBN-13: 978-1977044761
ISBN-10: 197704476X

Handouts, powerpoints, extracts, articles, links, reviews, news and revision materials available on www.peped.org

The peped.org website allows students and teachers to explore Philosophy of Religion and Ethics through handouts, film clips, presentations, case studies, extracts, games and academic articles.

Pitched just right, and so much more than a text book, here is a place to engage with critical reflection whatever your level. Marked student essays are also posted.

We also sell digital resources including Teaching Packs for the 2009 and 2016 specifications (full lesson plans, powerpoints, starter activities, and extracts for the entire course), marked essay packs, and a booklet giving full guidelines on how to answer questions on our summer exam paper predictions.

Contents

1. Philosophical Language and Thought 1

  1.1 Ancient Philosophical Influences 1

    Key Terms 1

    Specification 2

  1.1.1 The Philosophical Influences Of Plato.................................2

    A. Understanding of Reality...2

    B. Theory of FORMs..3

    C. The Allegory of the Cave...4

    D. Evaluation 5

  1.1.2 The Philosophical Influences Of Aristotle..........................7

    A. Understanding of Reality...7

    B. Four Causes 7

    C. Prime Mover 8

    D. Evaluation..9

    Confusions to Avoid 10

    Key Quotes 11

    Suggested Reading..11

    Practise Exam Question...11

    Possible Future Questions 12

  1.2 Soul, Mind And Body 13

    Key terms 13

    Specification 13

  1.2.1 The Thinking Of Plato And Aristotle 14

    A. Platonic Dualism 14

    B. Aristotelian Monism 16

    C. Evaluation..17

  1.2.2 Metaphysics Of Consciousness..19

    A. Substance Dualism 19

    B. Materialism..20

C. Evaluation...21

Confusions to Avoid 22

Key Quotes 23

Suggested Reading..24

Practise Exam Question...24

Possible Future Questions 25

2. Arguments for the Existence of God 27

2.1 Arguments Based On Experience 27

Key Terms 27

Specification 28

2.1.1 The Teleological Argument....................................28

A. Aquinas' Fifth Way...28

B. Paley's Teleological Argument...................................29

C. Evaluation..30

2.1.2 The Cosmological Argument 31

A. Aquinas' First, Second and Third Way 31

B. Evaluation 33

2.1.3 Challenges To The Arguments From Observation 34

A. Hume's Challenge against the Teleological Argument....34

B. Hume's Challenge against the Cosmological Argument ..35

C. The Challenge of Evolution..36

D. Evaluation..37

Confusions to Avoid 38

Key Quotes 38

Suggested Reading..39

Practise Exam Question...40

Possible Future Questions 41

2.2 Arguments Based In Reason....................................41

Key Terms 41

Specification 42

2.2.1 The Ontological Argument.....................................42

A. Anselm's First & Second Version................................42

B. Gaunilo's Response 43

C. Evaluation..44

Confusion to Avoid 46

Key Quotes 46

Suggested Reading..47

Practise Exam Question...47

Possible Future Questions 48

3. God and the World 49

3.1 Religious Experience..49

Key Terms 49

Specification 50

3.1.1 The Nature And Influence Of Religious Experience 50

A. Examples of Mystical Religious Experiences 50

B. Conversion experiences..52

C. Conclusions of William James 52

D. Evaluation...54

3.1.2 Different Ways In Which Religious Experience Can Be

Understood 56

A. Union with a great power.......................................56

B. Psychological affect 56

C. Product of physiological effect 57

D. Evaluation...58

Confusion to Avoid 59

Key Quotes 59

Suggested Reading..60

Practise Exam Question...60

Possible Future Questions 61

3.2 The Problem Of Evil 61

Key Terms 61

Specification 62

3.2.1 The Problem Of Evil And Suffering 62

A. Logical Aspects of the Problem 62

B. Evidential Aspects of the Problem 63

3.2.2 The Theodicies..64

A. Augustine's Theodicy 64

B. Hick's Theodicy..65

C. Evaluation...67

Confusion to Avoid 69

Key Quotes 69

Suggested Reading...70

Practise Exam Question...70

Possible Future Questions 71

4. Nature of God..73

Key Terms 73

Specification 74

4.1 Omnipotence 74

A. Evidence 74

B. Interpretations 75

4.2 Benevolence 77

A. Hell 77

B. Judgement 77

4.3 Omniscience 78

A. Unlimited Knowledge..78

B. Limited Knowledge 78

4.4 Eternity 79

A. Timeless..79

B. Four Dimentionalist Approach 80

C. Everlasting..81

4.5 Free Will 81

A. Boethius' Dilemma 81

B. Alternative Responses 82

Confusions to Avoid 82

Key Quotes 83

Suggested Reading...83

Practise Exam Question...84

Possible Future Questions 85

5. Classical Religious Language.......................................87

Key Terms...87

Specification 88

5.1 The Apophatic Way 89

A. Speaking with Certainty..89

B. Moses Maimonides 89

C. Teresa of Avila 90

D. Evaluation...91

Strengths of the Apophatic Way 91

5.2 The Cataphatic Way 92

A. The need for Analogy 92

B. Analogy of Attribution 93

C. Analogy of Proportionality 93

D. Evaluation...94

5.3 Symbolism 95

A. What are Signs and Symbols? 95

B. Paul Tillich on Signs and Symbols 96

C. The use of Symbols in Scripture and Religious Language 97

D. Evaluation...98

Confusions to Avoid 99

Key Quotes 100

Suggested Reading..100

Practise Exam Question...101

Possible Future Questions 102

6. Twentieth Century Perspectives on Religious Language.................103

Key Terms...103

Specification 104

6.1 Logical Positivism 104

A. The Principle of Verification 104

B. Ayer's Variations of the Principle of Verification 105

6.2 Wittgenstein's Language Games 107
    A. Language as a Form of Life 107
    B. Meaningful not Cognitive 108
6.3 Falsification Symposium 110
    A. Falsification 110
    B. Bliks 111
    C. Falsification Parables 112
    Confusions to Avoid 113
    Key Quotes 114
    Suggested Reading..115
    Practise Exam Question....................................115
    Possible Future Questions 116
    Exam Rescue Remedy..116
Postscript...119

1. Philosophical Language and Thought

1.1 Ancient Philosophical Influences

Key Terms

ALLEGORY - A story where the characters and events have a deeper hidden meaning

CAUSE - The reason why something exists

DOXA – Opinion (Greek); according to Plato we gain only opinion from experience

EFFICIENT - The agent or agents that **cause** something else to exist

EPISTEME – Knowledge (Greek); according to Plato we gain knowledge through reason, but according to Aristotle we gain knowledge through experience

ETERNAL - That which is timeless and unchanging

FORMS - Or theory of Ideas argues that non-physical (but substantial) **Forms** (or ideas) represent the most accurate reality. When used in this sense, the word form or idea is often capitalised.

GOOD - Not needing improvement

NECESSARY - The belief that the Prime Mover cannot not exist

TELOS - The final end of things, what they are made to do, the reason why they are brought into being

Specification

1.1 Ancient Philosophical Influences	1.1.1 The Philosophical Influences of Plato	A. Understanding of Reality B. Theory of FORMs C. Analogy of the Cave D. Evaluation
	1.1.2 The Philosophical Influences of Aristotle	A. Understanding of Reality B. Four Causes C. Prime Mover D. Evaluation

1.1.1 The Philosophical Influences Of Plato

A. Understanding of Reality

Plato believed that **EPISTEME** (true knowledge) could only come from a rational understanding of the **FORMS** as opposed to an experiential understanding of the world. Thus, Plato was a rationalist as opposed to an empiricist.

Plato was heavily influenced by Socrates, his teacher, who said that true knowledge came from knowing you know nothing. This means that you can know nothing from the world.

Plato believed that, given that the world was constantly changing, as Heraclitus demonstrated in his thought experiment about the river (you can never step in the same river twice); there was no certain knowledge that you could gain from the world.

Plato was also influenced by Pythagoras who suggested that there was a constant truth that existed in the world of ideas, e.g. mathematics, which never changed.

B. Theory of FORMs

Plato's **THEORY OF FORMS** stipulates that all things that we experience in this world are poor imitations of the true Forms, which exist abstractly in the World of FORMS. Plato argued that when we experience particulars, e.g. trees, cats, acts of affection etc. we are in fact experiencing a fleeting and changing example. Through the example we are "recognising" a true FORM. E.g. when I see oak and pine and ash, I am seeing examples of the true FORM of tree.

FORMs, then, are abstract ideas that have no physical existence. They are ideas that exist I the ethereal world or the world of ideas/FORMs. We can never experience them directly in this life, only recognise them through the particulars, the physical objects we encounter in this life.

The theory of FORMs postulates that there is an **ESSENTIAL** FORM of the good, which is the highest of all FORMs. It is through this Essential FORM that we can recognise the FORMs at all. It is this Essential FORM, which gives us any concept of goodness; things are good if they reflect the Essential FORM of the good through their FORM and bad if they do not. The clearer the good shines through, the closer the example is to the FORM and the better it is.

For example, the idea of chair-ness is reflected into an example of a new and comfortable chair. **GOODNESS** is shining clearly through the new chair such that the example is a close reflection of the FORM of chair. However, over time and misuse the chair becomes squeaky, torn and broken such that no longer is much goodness shining through the FORM so the example is old and broken and no longer a clear reflection of the FORM of chair. However, the FORM of chair never changes; it eternal as are all the Forms e.g. maths, love, justice. They are all **ETERNAL** and cannot change.

3

Justice is a FORM of knowing right from wrong. For Plato, if goodness shines through you, you are good, like the chair, you are a clear reflection of the FORM of man and the Essential FORM of Good is being shone through the FORM into you.

If you are a tyrant, then you are bad reflection.

C. The Allegory of the Cave

Plato presents the **ALLEGORY OF THE CAVE** in the Republic to illustrate that experience can only give us **DOXA** (opinion) and that **EPISTEME** (true knowledge) can only come through the knowledge of the FORMS.

The allegory that Plato resents goes as follows:

Prisoners are chained in a cave where they have been since birth and have only ever seen a wall on which shadows appear, caused by puppets being carried behind them. When they hear noises, they assume that these noises originate from the shadows as this is all they have ever known. When one of the prisoners is freed and takes the journey up the jagged path into the sunlight, at first, he will not understand what he sees as he is used to life in the cave. However, given time, his sight will adjust and he will realise that what he now sees, the puppets, the world etc. is the reality, given life by the sun, and that what he experienced in the cave was the illusion. Further, Plato suggests that if the freed prisoner where to venture back into the cave with tales of what is real outside the cave, his former fellow prisoners would reject what he says and will try to kill him.

Symbols of the Cave:

- **THE CAVE** - The physical world of experiences in which we are born, live and die

- **THE PRISONERS** - Normal people who experience the world and take what they experience as reality

- **THE SHADOWS** - Things that we sense in the world through sight,

4

hearing, taste etc.

- **THE PUPPETS** - The Forms which exist in a temporal world of ideas; they are the ideas that we recognise in the things we experience, e.g. love, truth, beauty etc.

- **THE JAGGED PATH** - The journey of the philosopher from ignorance to knowledge

- **THE SUN** - The Essential **FORM** of Goodness which is the highest of all Forms and is responsible for giving life to all things and through which all other Forms can be known

The **ALLEGORY** teaches us that while we think we are gaining knowledge from the physical world, we are in fact learning nothing but opinion, which is constantly changing.

In the same way that the prisoners are chained in the cave and only experience the **SHADOWS** on the wall, we are chained to our reality and only experience the temporal particulars of this physical world. In the same way that the free prisoner gains true knowledge by being freed from his restraints, crawling up the jagged path and seeing how the puppets cast shadows on the wall, we must free ourselves from our reliance on this world, become philosophers and accept that the truth lies in the abstract **FORMS** and that only then can we see the truth.

D. Evaluation

Strengths

Plato's theory of **FORMS** is supported by theories of a number of thinkers who were alive around the time of Plato, including:

1. **DEMOCRITUS**: He argued that all matter in the universe could be divided constantly until we come to the non-divisibles, things that could not be divided any more. In Greek, non-divisibles are called a-toms. In the 20th Century scientists thought they had found these and called them

atoms, but it turned out they were wrong. So, reason recognised an idea that experience failed to uncover.

2. **HERACLITUS**: He argued that the world is in constant flux meaning that it was constantly changing. The famous quote: *"you can never step in the same river twice"* highlights this view. So, experience gives only changing opinions; the world is like the river, constantly changing and we can gain no absolute truth from it.

3. **PARMENIDES**: He suggested that if you take a snapshot image of an arrow flying you will see that at any given point the arrow is stationary. This suggested to Plato that the **ETERNAL** world is fixed and unchanging.

4. **PYTHAGORAS**: Pythagoras' theorem suggests that some things are true abstractly and are ideas that exist ethereally and are unchanging. So, some things are unchanging and exist eternally, the **FORMS**.

Weaknesses

1. **THIRD MAN ARGUMENT**: Plato says that the 'FORM of man' is still a man. Therefore, if all men need a 'FORM of man', and the 'FORM of man' is also a man, then the men and the 'FORM of man' together need a FORM, which we might call the 'FORM of man+'. But the 'FORM of man+' is itself a man and needs a FORM, so the series continues ad infinitum.

2. **EXTENT OF THE WORLD OF FORMS**: It seems bizarre to think of such Forms existing eternally. If would suggest that there are Forms of every conceivable past present and future concept, even things that have not been invented yet and things that are clear negations of things.

1.1.2 The Philosophical Influences Of Aristotle

A. Understanding of Reality

Aristotle was Plato's student but inherently disagreed with Plato's understanding of reality. Where Plato was a pure **RATIONALIST**, Aristotle was an **EMPIRICIST**. He used a rational approach to understanding the world but believed that the only things we could know about the world came from the world itself.

Aristotle was preoccupied with **TELEOLOGY,** the causes of things. He believed that if you understood the causes of things you understood the thing. But this is not limited to what brings things about, but also what they are for.

B. Four Causes

Aristotle suggested that all things have four causes: these are the material, formal, **efficient** and final causes.

1. **MATERIAL** cause – The materials that make a thing. All things are made of material that could be a variety of different things, like wood, metal or wax. The material **cause** is the basic materials that make up anything. Some things are made of one material and others are a compound of many materials.

2. **FORMAL** cause – What a thing is. All things come in a raw state, like a block of wax or iron ore, and are then worked into a particular form. Some objects are formed from many different materials, but all things have a form. Everything is a form of something, e.g. the form of pencil, the form of candle or the form of computer.

3. **EFFICIENT** cause – The agent that brings a thing about. A block of marble stone is actually a block of marble stone with a potential to

7

become a statue. It must be moved from that potential state to the actual state of being a statue by an agent or agents who themselves may be using tools to make this reduction possible. This agent or agents that move the marble block into the statue are the **efficient** cause or causes.

4. **FINAL** cause – What a thing is made to do, its purpose or **TELOS**. Everything exists for a reason and that reason is the final cause, the ultimate end for any object within its actual state. Objects in a raw state, e.g. iron ore have no man-made purpose as they are naturally occurring but may well have a natural purpose unknown to us. Living objects like trees and animals have their own purposes to survive and reproduce. Everything has a purpose and we know more when we learn what things are for. For example, the appendix in the human body was believed to have no purpose, however, now we understand that it serves a vital function to house good bacteria.

C. Prime Mover

The theory of causes postulates Aristotle's theory of a Prime Mover. If all things are made of matter in a particular form, then the world itself is also made of material with a form. Motion is the reduction from **POTENTIALITY** (the raw material) to **ACTUALITY** (what it actually is, its form). Therefore, the world must have move from a potential state into its actual state towards some **TELOS** (final cause), the **PRIME MOVER**, which itself allows all motion to take place at all. The Prime Mover is not the **EFFICIENT** cause of the universe as every efficient cause is affected by what it moves, but the Prime Mover cannot be moved or changed. Instead, the Prime Mover is like the sun attracting the flower towards it; the sun attracts the flower but the flower does not affect the sun.

Aristotle presented a number of characteristics of the Prime Mover, for example:

- **PURE ACTUALITY** – The Prime Mover cannot itself be moved otherwise it cannot be the Prime Mover but one of a number of moved things.

- **SIMPLE** – Given that it is pure actuality, the Prime Mover cannot be a complex being like humans, as complexity implies complex form and motion.

- **GOOD** – The Prime Mover cannot change and so cannot be improved. This being the case, the Prime Mover must be perfect, incapable of improving, and so must be perfectly good.

D. Evaluation

Strengths

1. **EMPIRICAL:** Aristotle's approach has been adopted as the basic empirical approach to science and the development in understanding the world. By analysing the causes of things we can learn what things are and why they behave the way they do. It is the basis of what is called the scientific method.

2. **PROGRESS**: The Aristotelian approach is the basis of the scientific method. The scientific method is to experience the world, observe it, make hypothesis of how things work, test them and revise our hypothesis. Sometimes this process revolutionises how we think about ourselves: the sun no longer orbits the earth (Copernican revolution) and the Darwinian revolution suggests humankind evolved, rather than being created by God from 'the dust of the ground' (as in Genesis 1 & 2).

3. **EXPERIENTIAL**: Experience is the only tool we have as everything we do in life relies on our experiences, from the first instincts to reach for our mothers to our desires to travel and build space ships.

4. **REASONABLE**: If we think rationally about Plato's and Aristotle's theories of knowledge, there is far more that we can relate to in Aristotle's approach. It is more rational as it does not exclude experience.

Weaknesses

1. **UNRELIABLE**: Aristotle's observations were the first steps in our understanding of many things including medicine and technology, however, he himself made incorrect observations about things that could easily be discerned, e.g. his belief that women had fewer teeth than men and that some humans were born to be slaves.

2. **SUPERIORITY OF REASON**: The example of Democritus and the a-toms exemplifies the problem of experience as a substitute for reason. Reason can consider abstract ideas in a way that experience simply cannot.

3. **FALLACY OF INFERENCE**: When postulating the existence of the Prime Mover, Aristotle infers its existence from the four causes. However, as David Hume later argued, you cannot infer a causal connection between two things without direct experience.

Confusions to Avoid

1. Plato's Theory of Forms and the Allegory of the Cave are part of Plato's **THEORY OF KNOWLEDGE.** If a question asks about the **FORMS**, the Allegory can be used to support and justify what the Forms are. Likewise, if the question is about the Allegory, the question expects some explanation of what it was told to explain, that being the Forms themselves.

2. Do not confuse Aristotle's **FORMAL** cause with Plato's FORMS. Plato's Forms are **ABSTRACT IDEAS** that give rise to all things that we experience in the world. The FORM of tree for Plato is the tree-ness we recognise in the various examples of trees that we encounter in the world. However, for Aristotle, upon encountering various different trees, oak, elm, ash etc. we see the similarities and then label those different examples with a similar form by a term, i.e. tree. Aristotle's method is **A POSTERIORI**, from observation and experience.

Key Quotes

"There are certain forms, whose names these other things have through getting a share of them - as, for instance, just and beautiful has a share of justice and beauty." – Plato

"You cannot step in the same river twice." – Heraclitus

"True knowledge comes from knowing you know nothing." – Socrates

"There is not a third man or horse besides the ideal and the individuals" – Aristotle

Suggested Reading

Plato, Republic, Book V

Aristotle, Physics, Book 2 Part 3

Aristotle, Metaphysics, Book V

Practise Exam Question

Critically compare Plato's Form of the Good with Aristotle's Prime Mover.

AO1 Demonstrate knowledge and understanding through the use of some of the following material. (Maximum 16 marks)

- Outline Plato's explanation for the Essential **FORM** of **GOOD**, linked to his theory of FORMS and how it appears in the allegory of the cave.

- Show how the Essential FORM of GOOD is essential to our understanding of the FORMS and our understanding of goodness and badness.

- Outline Aristotle's explanation for the Prime Mover, postulated by the theory of the **FOUR CAUSES**.

- Show the characteristics of the **PRIME MOVER** and how it is completely abstract and cannot be acted upon but is pure actuality.

AO2 Demonstrate evaluation and analysis through the use of some of the following arguments (maximum 24 marks)

- Identify the strengths of Plato's Essential FORM of GOOD, including how it is part of Plato's **RATIONAL APPROACH** supported by Heraclitus' and Pythagoras' theories.

- Identify the weaknesses of Plato's Essential FORM of GOOD by outlining how it depends on the success of Plato's theory of FORMS, which itself has weaknesses including the **THIRD MAN FALLACY**.

- Identify the strengths of Aristotle's' Prime Mover, including how it is part of a rational and **EMPIRICAL** approach to understanding.

- Identify the weaknesses of Aristotle's Prime Mover, including how it is **INFERRED** without evidence.

- Compare both theories by identifying which has more strengths and weaknesses. This can be done by considering the success and failure of the theories to which they belong, i.e. Plato's and Aristotle's understandings of **REALITY**.

Possible Future Questions

1. Analyse Aristotle's four causes.

2. Critically assess Aristotle's understanding of the world.

3. Assess the claim that Plato does not value experience enough.

4. 'Plato's Theory of Forms explains how we know what we know.' Discuss

1.2 Soul, Mind And Body

Key terms

ANIMA - In Aristotle's De Anima, the anima is the soul of a person

DUALISM - the idea that mind and body are distinct substances

HYLOMORPHIC SOUL/BODY UNITY - Aristotle's interpretation of **MONISM**, that the body and soul are a unity and cannot be separated from each other (Greek, HYLE = form, MORPHE = matter)

IDENTITY THEORY - The theory that all mental activities including emotion and intelligence are centred in the brain

MATERIALISM - the idea that mind and body can be explained by physical or material interactions

MONISM - The belief that the body and soul are one and the same and that the soul cannot exist independently of the body

TRIPARTITE NATURE OF THE SOUL - In Platonic **DUALISM**, the belief that the soul is made of three parts: reason, spirit and appetite

Specification

1.2 Soul, Mind and Body	*1.2.1 The thinking of Plato and Aristotle*	*A. Platonic Dualism* *B. Aristotelian Monism* *C. Evaluation*
	1.2.2 Metaphysics of Consciousness	*A. SUBSTANCE dualism* *B. MATERIALISM* *C. Evaluation*

1.2.1 The Thinking Of Plato And Aristotle

A. Platonic Dualism

1. In Phaedrus

Plato presents the analogy of the charioteer to illustrate the **TRIPARTITE** nature of the soul:

- **THE BLACK HORSE**: Represents appetite, the lowest part of the soul linked to the role of the workers in Plato's perfect society. The appetite is the part of the soul that desires, craves and motivates. It is centred in the abdomen and leads to self-destructive craving.

- **THE WHITE HORSE**: Represents Spirit, the emotive part of the soul linked to the role of the auxiliaries in Plato's perfect society. The emotive soul is the part of the soul that is brave, emotional and fights. It is centred in the breast and leads to emotive conflict.

- **THE CHARIOTEER**: Represents reason, the highest part of the soul linked to the role of the guardian in Plato's perfect society. The rational soul is the part of the soul that thinks, reflects and learns. It is centred in the brain leads to balance.

If it can be demonstrated that people's behaviour reflects the tripartite soul, then it can be argued that the soul exists as a separate entity to the body and as such that we have a dualistic nature: body and soul separate. This does not in itself prove the immortality of the soul.

2. In Republic

Plato presented a version of the **MYTH** of **ER**, a soldier who died in battle but whose body did not decompose. Instead his soul went to the plane where the dead go and he witnessed the souls of his comrades being judged and going to different destinations, some into the sky and some into the ground. Additionally, he witnessed souls emerging from the sky, having been rewarded, and the ground, having been punished, and then choosing new lives before drinking from the river of forgetfulness only to be born again.

This process myth was borrowed from the **REINCARNATION** beliefs of Pythagoras. Plato called it transmigration of the soul, as the soul moved from one body to another. When in the ethereal plane, not only were they punished or rewarded, but they also gained all knowledge of the **FORMS** before forgetting it all again only to be born. This belief explains the Plato's view of how the soul is distinguished from the body and can exist independently.

3. In Phaedo

Plato presents his four arguments for life after death:

1. **ARGUMENT FROM OPPOSITES**: All things are in constant motion between two extremes, e.g. all different temperatures are a flux between hot and cold; all different lengths are a flux between long and short. All opposites are extremes and Heraclitus' LOGOS was what prevented any extreme being surpassed. We can observe these opposites in life and so we can be certain of them. In the same way, then, life must have its opposite in death. In the same way that things move from hot to cold and then to hot again we must accept that we move from life to death and then to life again.

2. **ARGUMENT FROM RECOLLECTION**: All knowledge comes from the FORMs, which are eternal ideas that we cannot experience. When we are in the World of FORMs in between lives we know them intimately, and then we forget about them. When on earth, our experiences are in fact us recollecting the FORMs that we see in the examples we encounter. When I see a tree I recollect tree-ness within it. This would only be possible if I already had possessed the knowledge of tree-ness from some previous existence. For Plato, this recollection is proof that we existed previously to our births from where we recall that knowledge.

3. **ARGUMENT FROM AFFINITY**: Plato identifies two kinds of existence, the physical and the non-physical. He shows how all things that we encounter physically have a non-physical affinity. For each tree, there is the non-physical tree-ness, for the act of affection there is the non-physical idea of affection. Likewise, for each life there is the non-physical self. Cebes challenges this by giving the example of the music played that ends when the instrument is destroyed, but Plato insists that the affinity of a person is an eternal affinity.

4. **ARGUMENT FROM THE THEORY OF FORMS**: For the theory of FORMs to work, as Plato insisted that it did, it was essential that the soul was eternal so that we can know the FORMs in the plane between worlds and then recognise them when we were incarnated. Without life before and after death, the theory of FORMs cannot work.

In these arguments, Plato is presenting his case for why life after death cannot be refuted but instead must be accepted as a reality. It is based in the nature of **DUALISM** and is embedded in the theory of the World of FORMS.

B. Aristotelian Monism

Aristotle presented his ideas concerning the soul in his work **DE ANIMA**. In the work, Aristotle discusses the nature of the relationship between the body and the soul all stemming from his earlier argument for the **FOUR CAUSES**. Aristotle argues that the body and soul make up a **HYLOMORPHIC** body/soul unity. For Aristotle, there is no separate soul, but rather, the soul is the form and purpose of the body, the body in action. This can be seen through his explanation of potentiality and actuality and then of cause and effect.

The human being is matter in some form fulfilling some **TELOS**. the soul is the **ACTUALITY** of the body. Aristotle gives the wax stamp example to emphasise the unity between the body and soul. The stamp cannot be removed from the wax as they are one unity. Likewise, whatever it is that makes the soul, the appearance, shape, character, personality etc. it is all part of the physical person; the soul is the form of the body, the actuality of the flesh, not something separate from it.

- First potentiality – our material self with the potential to fulfil some **TELOS**.

- Second potentiality/first actuality – our formal self with potential to enact a **TELOS**.

- Second actuality – our purpose being engaged fulfilling a **TELOS**.

The soul is **ANIMATION**, the person engaging with their purpose, which is determined by their form and doing what they are supposed to be doing. As Aristotle said, if an axe had a soul it would be chopping; if an eye had a soul it would be seeing. We have a soul, and that is to engage with reason and live the good life.

Therefore, there can be no question of the soul existing disembodied as the soul nothing more than the animation of the body. It is not a separate thing that can exist separately. The body and soul are a **HYLOMORPHIC** soul/body unity.

C. Evaluation

Strengths of Platonic Dualism

1. **ANTHONY KENNY** supported the idea that the psyche develops in his observation of the tantrums of toddlers. They know they crave and have the emotions to cry but have no intellect to know how to control those feelings.

2. In the same way we can support Plato's argument for the FORMS, we can support Plato's rational approach to the self and the **DUALISTIC PSYCHE**. Many would argue that there is a part of us that is separate from the body that makes our character.

3. Many eastern traditions have adopted reincarnation as part of their belief system. These can be used to support Plato's argument for the World of FORMS. In fact, the work of Dr **IAN STEVENSON** on reincarnation is modern scientific evidence to support the belief in reincarnation. He

recorded thousands of reincarnation accounts which, though not conclusive of anything, stand as evidence to support Plato's claims.

Weaknesses of Platonic Dualism

Plato's Argument from Opposites is in fact impossible to infer.

1. **EVIDENCE**: Plato's arguments of Opposites is impossible to infer. His arguments of Recollection, Affinity and the World of FORMs are all part of his theory of FORMS, which Aristotle challenged. If this theory of knowledge can be attacked it undermines the whole argument for Platonic dualism.

2. **HERESY**: Dualism is rejected by the Catholic Church and, as part of a Gnostic ideology, is considered heresy as it implies that the soul alone is good and the body is evil. The Catholic Catechism states that the soul is the FORM of the body and they were created, and are, one. "Because man is a composite being, spirit and body, there already exists a certain tension in him; a certain struggle of tendencies between "spirit" and "flesh" develops. But in fact this struggle belongs to the heritage of sin. It is a consequence of sin and at the same time a confirmation of it. It is part of the daily experience of the spiritual battle" Catechism 2516.

Strengths of Aristotelian Monism

1. **SCIENTIFIC**: Aristotle's interpretation of the soul as the animation of the body fits well with all modern scientific attitudes as the soul can be seen in light of the brain's activity and personal identity. It does not force the believer to accept an abstract world or a spiritual dimension.

2. **BIBLICAL**: John Hick supports Aristotle's **MONISM** when he argues that the only self we can know is the empirical self. He argues that God has made us as a psycho-somatic soul/body unity, and that the resurrection of Christ was a purely bodily resurrection. This is supported

by the letters of St Paul when he describes resurrection as being with a 'spiritual body'.

Weaknesses of Aristotelian Monism

1. **EVIDENCE**: Aristotle's **MONISM** is itself difficult to demonstrate beyond doubt. Aristotle did not give a clear indication if there was life after death. He seemed to have allowed for the possibility for the Prime Mover to maintain a person's intelligence but this was never developed.

1.2.2 Metaphysics Of Consciousness

A. Substance Dualism

For Descartes, the soul is a **SPIRITUAL** entity that resided within the body as a spiritual substance distinct from the physical substance that makes up the body. The soul exists throughout the body and operates in all parts of it. The part of the body, however, which was most associated with the operation of the soul, is the **PINEAL GLAND** in the base of the brain. From here, the soul moved the body around by way of directing the spirit through the ventricles and arteries and thus operating the body like some super marionette.

Descartes chose the pineal gland as, in his time, it was believed that the pineal gland otherwise had no purpose in the brain, and secondly because, while the rest of the brain was divisible into two halves, everything from the left mirroring everything on the right, the pineal gland appeared indivisible. In this way, Descartes was building an **ANATOMICAL** picture for the operations of the soul's interaction with the body.

One way of better understanding **DESCARTES**' view of the soul's interaction with the body is to compare it to the cardiovascular system (this is NOT an example given by Descartes).

System	The soul	Cardiovascular system
Substance that moves through the system	Spirit	Blood
Areas that the substance operates through	Pineal Gland	Heart
Function of the substance	Move the body	Takes energy/oxygen round the body

Descartes suggested that the distinction between the substance of the body and the soul was evident as it was possible to deny the existence of our bodies, but not to deny the existence of the self: "I think, therefore, I am".

B. Materialism

IDENTITY THEORY is a belief that a person's self-identity is linked directly to their physical body. It is a materialist approach formed from a series of scholarly ideas and beliefs:

JOHN LOCKE: This 17th Century philosopher presented the thought experiment of a prince and cobbler who wake up in each other's bodies. When he wakes up, the prince presents himself to the palace but is sent out as he appears as the cobbler. The thought experiment asks us to consider what the person is: the physical body or the consciousness.

PHINEAS GAGE: He was a 19th Century railroad construction foreman who suffered the fate of having a metal pole through his brain. While he survived, he was forever changed as a person, from being approachable and friendly, to being short tempered and easily angered. This suggests that the character of a person, or their soul, is directly linked to the physical brain itself, not some spiritual substance.

GILBERT RYLE: This 20th Century philosopher rejected the notion that the soul and body were distinct, taking a position particularly in opposition to Descartes by arguing that he committed a **CATEGORY ERROR** in which he categorises the body as one type of stuff and the soul as another. He gives an example of a visitor at Oxford who asks to see the university and is guided around the campus and sees the dorms, the registry office, the fields etc. But then he asks "where is the university?" It is a category error to think that the university is more than the sum of its parts. In the same way Descartes is wrong to think that the person is more than the sum of its body. There is no other self or soul that makes the person.

RICHARD DAWKINS: The contemporary atheist argues that the body is a survival machine for the genes which survive within us. They last forever if they are successful and they determine everything about our character and person. We should, therefore, not consider ourselves special in any particular way as we are governed by our genes and the idea of a life after death is simply a MEME that our brains have created in order to cope with the reality of our fate. He identified that there are two definitions of a soul:

> Soul 1: The traditional idea of a soul that exists separately.
> Soul 2: The mind and character of a person.

C. Evaluation

Strengths of Substance Dualism

1. **SUPPORTS PLATONIC DUALISM** – Substance Dualism supports Plato's dualism and helps us to see how the body and soul can interact in a measurable way.

Weaknesses of Substance Dualism

1. **UNSCIENTIFIC**: The reality is that much of Descartes' ideas were demonstrated to be false and in fact poor science. The pineal gland is the

part of the brain that secretes Melatonin and in no way can it house or direct a soul.

2. **HOMUNCULUS FALLACY**: Descartes commits the homunculus fallacy in that the argument that the soul directs the body leaves us with a similar problem - to explain what drives the soul itself.

Strengths of Materialism

1. **PSYCHOLOGY**: **IDENTITY THEORY** can be demonstrated by observing how people's behaviour is affected by psychology and a physiology. When we observe people's characters changing on account of drugs and alcohol we are witnessing a change to the character which supports the idea that the soul is in fact the character formed by the physical brain.

2. **MOTIVATION**: Stephen Davis argued that Identity theory only explains the workings of the brain, and not the motivation of the brain. He discusses the brain may be neutral and that the soul is what guides it.

3. **THE BRAIN**: The reality is that know little about the brain and how it actually works, so everything we claim about how the brain works and how interacts with the body and forms the character is pure speculation.

Confusions to Avoid

1. The analogy of the **CHARIOTEER** does not describe how the psyche drives the body. The charioteer is not the psyche and the chariot is not the body. The charioteer and horses are the whole psyche in its tripartite nature (**REASON, SPIRIT** and **APPETITE**).

2. Plato's **DUALISM** might be improbable/unprovable; it is not inconsistent. Following Plato's reasoning it is acceptable to conclude the existence of the World of FORMS. To undermine the whole you need to attack dualism, or the arguments for the Theory of FORMS. Similarly, we cannot prove reincarnation. Given the nature of the spiritual realm you

would never be able to, so absence of evidence is not evidence of absence.

3. Aristotle was a **MONIST**, not a **MATERIALIST**. Materialist approaches, including **IDENTITY THEORY**, are suppositions and speculations, not proofs. It would be wrong to assume that it has proven anything concrete about the nature of the body and soul. In fact, there is arguably more evidence for REINCARNATION than Identity theory, both from the number of believers to the work of Dr **IAN STEVENSON** (see Strengths of Dualism).

Key Quotes

"The body is the source of endless trouble to us by reason of the mere requirement of food; and is liable also to disease which overtake and impede us in the search after true being." – Plato

"Which person was which? Is it the mind that makes the individual, or the body? What makes us what we are? Is it our appearance, our memories, our individual personality traits, or is it something else?" – John Locke

"'the dogma of the Ghost in the Machine'...I hope to prove that it is entirely false, and false not in detail but in principle." – Gilbert Ryle

"Compared the human to a river, once the water is gone from the bed what is left of the river?" – Bertrand Russell

"After some disaster when the 'Dead' and the 'Survivors' have both been listed, what logical space is left for a third category, 'Both'?" – Anthony Flew

"God didn't promise Abraham eternal life as an individual. But he did promise him something else...God knew Darwinism." – Richard Dawkins

Suggested Reading

Aristotle, De Anima, Book II Part 1

Richard Dawkins' The Selfish Gene Chapter 3

Descartes Principles of Philosophy, Part 1, LX. Of distinctions; and first of the real.

Gilbert Ryle, The Concept of Mind, Ch. 1: Descartes' Myth, Part 5

Practise Exam Question

Assess the claim that disembodied existence is possible.

AO1 Demonstrate knowledge and understanding through the use of some of the following material. (Maximum 16 marks)

- Outline the Platonic dualist position including Plato's Charioteer example.

- Explain Plato's four arguments for life after death. Include the example of the Myth of Er.

- Outline Aristotle's monist position, including his view that the soul is the actuality of the body. Use the example of the wax stamp.

AO2 Demonstrate evaluation and analysis through the use of some of the following arguments (maximum 24 marks)

- Support Plato's dualism with Descartes' Substance Dualism position including his argument that that the soul operates through the pineal gland and that we cannot deny our selves.

- Support Plato's position with reference to the research of Dr Ian Stevenson to support reincarnation.

- Support Aristotle's monist position with John Hick's view that the only self we can know is the empirical self.

- Support Aristotle's position with the materialist position that rejects the view that the soul is distinct.

- Outline the strengths and weaknesses of each position.

- Compare Plato's and Aristotle's views and draw a conclusion.

Possible Future Questions

1. 'There is no such thing as a soul.' Discuss.

2. To what extent does Plato successfully explain the relationship between the body and the soul?

3. 'The body and soul cannot be separated.' Discuss.

4. Evaluate what Aristotle meant by arguing that the soul is the form of the body.

2. Arguments for the Existence of God

2.1 Arguments Based On Experience

Key Terms

ACTUALITY – When something is in the state of doing something; what a thing is, e.g. fire is actually hot.

ANALOGY - A comparison between two things using one to infer conclusions of the other

CONTINGENT - Something that does not need to exist, it depends on something else to exist

NECESSARY - Something that cannot not be the case

POTENTIALITY – When something has the power to be something else, e.g. wood is potentially hot.

TELOS - (Greek) purpose

Specification

2.1 Arguments based in Observation	2.1.1 Teleological Argument	A. Aquinas' Fifth Way B. Paley's teleological argument C. Evaluation
	2.1.2 Cosmological Argument	A. Aquinas' First three ways B. Evaluation
	2.1.3 Challenges to the arguments from observation	A. Hume's challenges of the arguments from observation B. The challenge of evolution

2.1.1 The Teleological Argument

A. Aquinas' Fifth Way

St Thomas Aquinas presented his fifth way to prove God's existence a posteriori in the Summa Theologica as the argument from the Governance of the World:

1. Things that lack intelligence act for an **END**. Things such as natural bodies all act towards some end, e.g. planets orbit stars, plants grow towards the sun and seasons change etc.

2. All things act as if **DESIGNED**. Everything works towards its end as though it were designed this way.

3. Things that lack knowledge are directed by things with **INTELLIGENCE**. Aquinas gives the example of the archer. The arrow cannot direct itself and so is directed to its mark by the archer.

4. Some intelligent being exists to direct all things to their goals. Since everything in the universe moves towards its **PURPOSE** (telos) and cannot direct itself, there must be an intelligence that directs these things by governing the universe and moving all things towards their prescribed goals.

5. This is what we call God. Aquinas is arguing that there is a **SUPREME INTELLIGENCE**. He is then stating the God of Christian faith is in fact this supreme intelligence.

B. Paley's Teleological Argument

William Paley presented his version of the Teleological Argument in his book **NATURAL THEOLOGY**. This was written after David Hume presented his challenges to the teleological argument and so was likely unaware of them. Paley was a biologist of his time and so his arguments are based on observation of nature.

Paley argued that all things are **FIT FOR PURPOSE**. All natural bodies are suitably designed for their purposes. He drew this conclusion by observing the natural world, particularly natural organisms, e.g. pigs' teats are sufficient for feeding a litter; swans' necks are long enough to reach the bottom of ponds; and the eye is perfectly fit for seeing.

If all things were fit for purpose and appeared designed for their purposes, then that design denoted a **DESIGNER**. If something is perfectly designed to fulfil a purpose, it suggests that there is a designer who designed it for that purpose.

Paley presented the **ANALOGY** of the watch, where he suggested that if one find a watch on a beach they would immediately conclude that there was a watchmaker. In the same way, upon reflection of the human being and the physical world, we should similarly conclude that there is a designer God.

C. Evaluation

Strengths of the Teleological Argument

1. The **TELEOLOGICAL ARGUMENT** includes any observation of nature that leaves us no explanation for its existence other than God. Anthony Flew, following a lifetime of atheism, was finally converted to theism following the reflection of the double helix within DNA. He could no longer deny that the incredible complexity of DNA had no explanation other than God.

2. **PAUL DAVIES** argued in The Mind of God that science has allowed us to better understand the world, and in so doing has allowed us to see how we are connected to an intricate universe. This beauty denotes pattern and intention.

Weaknesses of the teleological argument

1. **MALEVOLENCE**: John Stuart Mill argued in On Nature that if there was a designer of the world, then this designer is either malevolent or stupid to create a world with such natural evil within it. Jean Paul Sartre argued similarly when he discussed this imperfect world. If there is natural evil in a designed world, then it is accountable to the designer.

2. **CIRCULAR REASONING**: Richard Swinburne argued in The Essence of God that Aquinas' argument committed the fallacy of begging the question. This is a factor in all teleological arguments where the premises infer design. If a designer is inferred in the premises then the conclusion – the world has a designer – is assumed before it is proven.

3. **UNSCIENTIFIC**: Richard Dawkins argued in The Blind Watchmaker argued that, while Paley was working with the best knowledge of his time, he was utterly wrong as the appearance of the eye, the pigs' teats and the swan's neck can all be accounted for by evolution, not a designer.

2.1.2 The Cosmological Argument

A. Aquinas' First, Second and Third Way

St Thomas Aquinas presented his first three ways to prove God's existence a posteriori in the Summa Theologica. These form the Cosmological Argument:

1. First Way, From Motion

1. Everything is in a state of motion. This can be observed in the world, e.g. seasons change, plates move in orbits etc.

2. Motion is the reduction from **POTENTIALITY** to **ACTUALITY**, e.g. the wood is actually cold but has the potential of being actually hot and nothing can move itself. The wood cannot make itself hot; it must be moved into a state of heat by a source of heat, e.g. fire.

3. Motion cannot **REGRESS** infinitely. If there was no first motion, there would be no subsequent motion and therefore no current motion. But we observe motion.

4. There must be a **FIRST MOTION** that is itself unmoved. If the first motion were itself moved, then it would not be the first motion. Therefore, the first motion cannot itself be moved. It must be pure **ACTUALITY** and so unmoved.

5. This is what we call God. Aquinas is arguing that there is a **FIRST MOVER**. He is then stating the God of Christian faith is in fact this First Mover, not the other way round.

2. Second Way, From Causality

1. Everything is an **EFFECT** that is caused. We can observe cause and effect in our daily life, e.g. parents cause children to exist etc.

2. Nothing can cause itself. Everything must be caused by something that is not itself. Rather, things must be caused by something previous to itself.

3. Causation cannot regress infinitely. If there was no first cause, there would be no subsequent effects and therefore no current effects. But we observe cause and effect now.

4. There must be a **FIRST CAUSE** that is itself uncaused. If the first cause were itself caused, then it would not be the first cause. Therefore, the first cause cannot be caused. It must be pure cause and so uncaused.

5. This is what we call God. Aquinas is arguing that there is a First Cause. He is then stating the God of Christian faith is in fact this First Cause, not the other way round.

3. Third Way, From Necessity and Contingency

1. All things are **CONTINGENT** (exist because of the way the world happens to be). Everything we observe could potentially not exist; nothing necessarily exists in and of itself.

2. All things that exist contingently at one point did not exist. Allowing for an infinite amount of time, there could be a time when there was nothing in existence at all.

3. Nothing comes from nothing. If ever there was nothing, then, since nothing can come from nothing, there would be nothing at all. But evidently there is something.

4. There must be a **NECESSARY EXISTENCE**. In order to account for why there is something at all, we must accept that there is something that cannot not exist, but is necessary.

5. This is what we call God. Aquinas is arguing that there is a Necessary Being. He is then stating the God of Christian faith is in fact this Necessary Being, not the other way round.

B. Evaluation

Strengths of the Cosmological Argument

1. Aquinas' Cosmological Argument reflects Aristotle's four causes and his argument for the Prime Mover:

- All things are moved from their material cause (potentiality) to their formal cause (actuality). And so if you trace back all movement you must come to a Prime Mover (First Mover).

- All things have an efficient cause (cause) in order to achieve some final cause (effect). And so if you trace back all causes you must come to a Prime Mover (First Cause).

2. Fr Friedrich Copleston supported the cosmological argument by presenting his version of the argument from contingency in a radio debate with Bertrand Russell in 1948.

- Some things in the world are not the explanation for their own existence, e.g. we depend on our parents to exist and the air we breathe to continue existing.

- The world is the real or imagined aggregate of **CONTINGENT** things. There is no world separate from the aggregate of things in the world. And so nothing about the world explains the existence of it.

- We must look for a total explanation for all things. If we find it all well and good, if not we proceed further until we find a total explanation. This links to Gottfried Leibniz' argument for sufficient reason.

Weaknesses of the Cosmological Argument

1. **FALLACY OF INFERENCE**: Immanuel Kant argued in Transcendental Dialectic that the process of cause and effect are subjects of the universe and as such we can never infer that they work beyond this universe. For

this reason, we can never postulate what 'causes' this universe as we can never look beyond it.

2. **NECESSITY**: Bertrand Russell argued in his radio debate with Copleston that the terms used in the cosmological argument hold no meaning. Not only does necessary being mean nothing, and in fact reminded him of the ontological argument, but further, it makes no sense to discuss a total cause. It is enough to know that the striking of the match caused the flame without looking for a total explanation. For this reason, the cosmological argument goes too far in its assumption of what we can know from principles of cause and effect.

3. **PROBLEM OF DEISM**: Other problems with the cosmological argument include the problem of deism. The argument need not conclude that there is a theistic sustaining God, but rather a distant creator. Though Aquinas was cure to state that what we believed God to be was the First Mover. Still this is not proof, just faith.

4. **INFINITE REGRESSION**: One modern challenge responds to Aquinas' rejection of infinite regression. Modern physicists do not reject the possibility of infinite regression. Many discuss inflation rather than a big bang. It has not escaped them that Einstein's principle that energy cannot be created or destroyed. So how can you have something from nothing?

2.1.3 Challenges To The Arguments From Observation

A. Hume's Challenge against the Teleological Argument

David Hume presented his challenges against teleological arguments in general, not against any one particular argument. There are many challenges but these are the most succinct:

1. **FALLACY OF ANALOGY**: Analogy can only be used when comparing two similar things. When the world is compared to a **MACHINE** and it is inferred that the world must have a maker as the machine has a maker, this is a false use of analogy. He famously said that the world is more like a cabbage than a machine; not because the world is anything like a cabbage, but because it is evidently nothing like a machine.

2. **FALLACY OF INFERENCE**: Hume argued that just because there appeared to be ORDER in the world this does not mean that there is in fact order. This is to infer order where there is no proof of it. In fact, Hume argued, apparent order can come from actual chaos. Since 'order' is self-perpetuating, if all things started in chaos, then when order randomly appears then it maintains itself and we infer an order to it. Just because A then B, does not mean B then A.

3. **ASSUMPTION OF MONOTHEISM**: Hume argued that even if the teleological argument worked in proving that there was a designer God, there is no way that you can assume that there is one God. Hume used the example of the ship being built by many shipwrights to show that it is very possible that there may be **MANY GODS** who are responsible for the world for all we know.

B. Hume's Challenge against the Cosmological Argument

David Hume challenged the cosmological argument in Dialogues Concerning Natural Religion and various other writings. The following are three of the most direct challenges.

1. **LACK OF EXPERIENCE**: Hume pointed out that we have no experience of universes being created. All we can ever know of motion and cause and effect only comes from experience. Since we have never experienced the creation of universes, we can never discuss it with any kind of knowledge or certainty. This can be used to challenge the postulation that all things need movement or initial cause. Since **INFINITE**

REGRESSION is a theoretical possibility, and since we have never experienced the supposed 'initial motion/cause', we can never assume there is one.

2. **CAUSATION CANNOT BE OBSERVED**: Hume took this challenge from William of Ockham who presented this very challenge against Aquinas himself. The principle of causation itself cannot be experienced and so is assumed. Hume gives the example of the billiard balls. When we see one ball supposedly hitting the other, we are in fact making an **ASSUMPTION**. We never actually experience the connection and causation between them. We just assume it is happening. For all we know the two never touch, and in fact at an atomic level the do not! Additionally, when a man hails a bus, though it appears that he is stopping it, he in fact is not. In this way we can challenge Aquinas as causation is implied, never observed, and so the second way is undermined.

3. **'NECESSARY BEING' HAS NO LOGICAL MEANING**: This challenge was later picked up by Bertrand Russell as a challenge to the logic of the cosmological argument. When Aquinas discusses the idea of a necessary being that is required if there are contingent things, Hume challenges this as the term 'necessary being' has no meaning in itself. Russell supports this by arguing that the only necessary things are **ANALYTIC** propositions, like 'triangles have three sides'. Hume supports Kant's claim that all existential propositions are **SYNTHETIC** and so no being can ever be said to necessarily exist.

C. The Challenge of Evolution

Charles Darwin's book, the **ORIGIN OF SPECIES**, was a great challenge to the teleological argument as it presented a way of thinking about life in the universe without recourse to the biblical creation story and the idea that all life forms were created in the way that we see them.

The theory of evolution suggests that all life forms have evolved from simpler organisms through a process of natural selection. Darwin suggested that life forms undergo random mutations over millennia and that the mutations that better serve survival are the ones that remain.

Darwin gave the example of the finches found on the Galapagos Islands. Darwin found many variations of finches each, which were perfectly adapted to their environments and food sources. This suggested that creatures evolve from simpler organisms and adapt to survive.

This position is a particular challenge to teleological arguments such as William Paley's which depends on the idea that all forms of life are **FIT FOR PURPOSE**.

D. Evaluation

Weaknesses of the challenge of Evolution

1. **IRREDUCIBLE COMPLEXITY**: Michael **BEHE** in Darwin's Black Box argued that there are some things in the universe that are so complex that they cannot be reduced into a simpler predecessor. He gives various examples of this irreducible complexity, including the **FLAGELLUM** which he argues could not have evolved randomly. Evolution is a theory that organisms have changed over millennia from simpler organisms. Darwin said this worked by the principle of Natural Selection; however, this only works when you have a variety of variations that can be narrowed down, so the one that is the fittest survives. But what creates the variance is debatable. Richard Dawkins and other atheist biologists argue it is random mutation within species that give this variation. However, Behe's examples challenge this. If there is no way that the flagellum could have randomly appeared then it could not have been naturally selected. (Flagellum = a slender thread-like structure, especially a microscopic whip-like appendage which enables many protozoa, bacteria, spermatozoa, etc. to swim).

Confusions to Avoid

1. Aquinas was not discussing motion and causation back in time. He was not saying that the first motion or **FIRST CAUSE** were at the start of the universe. The understanding of fixed point creation and the expansion of time and space was not firmly argued scientifically until the 20th Century. Aquinas was referring to first motion and first cause within the universe now. He was describing the nature of a God that sustains the world now, not one that started the world 14 billion years ago.

2. David Hume wrote twenty-three years before William Paley, so his Dialogues Concerning Natural Religion are not a response to Paley's version of the teleological argument. Though it is tempting to see Hume's challenge as saying that the world is not like a watch, and that the world is more like a cabbage than a watch, this is utterly mistaken. Hume was more likely responding to the **NEWTONIAN MODEL** of the universe which saw it like a machine. Hume was challenging this mechanistic view, as one of his challenges to the cosmological argument was that we cannot experience **CAUSATION** and so we cannot infer this mechanical interpretation of the world.

Key Quotes

Teleological Argument

"Now whatever lacks intelligence cannot move towards an end, unless it be directed by some being endowed with knowledge and intelligence; as the arrow is shot to its mark by the archer." – St Thomas Aquinas

"This mechanism being observed, the inference we think is inevitable, that the watch must have had a maker." – William Paley

"We have no data to establish any system of cosmogony." – David Hume

"Aquinas' statement that all things are directed by some mind towards a purpose, and that mind is God, commits the fallacy of begging the question. Things need a

purpose, God gives things a purpose, therefore God must be the purpose." – Richard Swinburne

"Paley's argument is made with passionate sincerity and is informed by the best biological scholarship of the day, but it is wrong, gloriously and utterly wrong." – Richard Dawkins

Cosmological Argument

"Suppose the book of the elements of geometry to have been eternal, one copy always having been written down from an earlier one. It is evident that even though a reason can be given for the present book out of a past one, we should never come to a full reason." – Gottfried Leibniz

"Nothing is demonstrable, unless the contrary is a contradiction." – David Hume

"We find...the transcendental principle whereby from the contingent we infer a cause. This principle is applicable only in the sensible world; outside that world it has no meaning whatsoever." – Immanuel Kant

"This being is either itself the reason for its own existence, or it is not. If it is, well and good. If not, then we must proceed further. But if we proceed to infinity in that sense, then there's no explanation of existence at all." – Fr Friedrich Copleston

"The word "necessary" I should maintain, can only be applied significantly to propositions. And, in fact, only to such as are analytic -that is to say - such as it is self-contradictory to deny." – Bertrand Russell

Suggested Reading

St Thomas Aquinas, Summa Theologica Part 1, Question 2, Article 3

St Thomas Aquinas, Summa Theologica, Part 1, Question 2, Article 3

David Hume, A Treatise of Human Nature, Book 1 Part 3

Immanuel Kant, Transcendental Dialectic, Book II, Chapter III

Practise Exam Question

To what extent does Hume successfully argue that observation does not prove the existence of God?

AO1 Demonstrate knowledge and understanding through the use of some of the following material. (Maximum 16 marks)

- Briefly outline the teleological argument, including Aquinas' fifth way and Paley's argument.

- Briefly outline the cosmological argument, including an amalgamation of Aquinas' three ways or one of the ways in a little detail.

- Outline at least two of Hume's challenges against the Teleological Argument explaining one of them in detail.

- Outline at least two of Hume's challenges against the Cosmological Argument explaining one of them in detail.

AO2 Demonstrate evaluation and analysis through the use of some of the following arguments (maximum 24 marks)

- Present the defence for the teleological argument. You might include links to Aristotelian thinking and Behe's defence of irreducible complexity.

- Present the defence for the cosmological argument. You might include reference to Copleston and Russell's radio debate.

- Present support for Hume's position, including Kant's Transcendental Dialectic and Dawkins' response to Paley.

- Compare the arguments for and against the arguments from observation and draw a conclusion.

Possible Future Questions

1. 'The world was created by chance, not by God's design.' Discuss.

2. To what extent does Aquinas' cosmological argument successfully reach the conclusion that there is a transcendent creator?

3. 'Aquinas' fifth way does not demonstrate the existence of God.' Discuss.

4. Assess the claim that the cosmological argument proves that God exists a posteriori.

2.2 Arguments Based In Reason

Key Terms

A PRIORI - Before experience

A POSTERIORI - After experience

ANALYTIC - Self-evident knowledge, known **a priori**

CONTINGENT - Something that does not need to exist but depends on something else to exist

DE DICTO - By word/definition

DE RE - In reality/the real world

NECESSARY - Something that cannot not be the case

PREDICATE - The **predicate** is the part of a sentence (or clause) which tells us what the subject does or is eg God (subject) exists (**predicate**)

SYNTHETIC - Matters of fact, descriptions of how things are, known **a posteriori**

Specification

2.2 Arguments based in Reason	2.2.1 Ontological Argument	A. Anselm's Argument 1
		B. Anselm's Argument 2
		C. Gaunilo's Response

2.2.1 The Ontological Argument

A. Anselm's First & Second Version

Anselm sought to prove that God exists using reason alone. Influenced by Psalm 14: 'The fool has said in his heart "there is no God"', Anselm wanted to show that it was a matter of foolishness for anyone to know what God is and maintain that there is no God.

He therefore set out to demonstrate that God's existence can be proven **ANALYTICALLY**, as a matter of reason, from what we mean by God. He sought to prove that God existed necessarily and that this could be shown **A PRIORI**. He attempted to do this in two versions presented in Proslogion chapters 2 and 3.

Version 1

Premise 1: God is a being than which nothing greater can be conceived. When people discuss God, they know they are discussing the God of classical theism, not Zeus or Thor, but God which is all powerful, all good etc.

Premise 2: It is greater to exist in the mind and reality than the mind alone.

Anselm is implying that existence is a **PREDICATE** of God's nature.

Example: When a painter conceives of a painting, he has that idea in his mind but it is not yet in reality. When he paints it, he has it on the canvas and when he contemplates it now, the idea of the existing painting, compared to the idea of the paining before it was painted, is greater.

Conclusion: God must exist. If God only existed in the mind and not reality, he would not be the greatest possible being, as, theoretically, a God that did exist would be greater than a God that did not exist. Therefore, God, to be the greatest possible being, must exist in mind and reality.

Version 2

Premise 1: God is a being than which nothing greater can be conceived.

Premise 2: **Necessary** existence is greater than **CONTINGENT** existence. If we consider the relationship between necessary and contingent things, we find that **NECESSARY** things are greater as they cannot not exist, whereas contingent things depend on others and can conceivably not exist.

Conclusion: God must necessarily exist. If God is that than which nothing greater can be conceived, and necessary existence is greater than contingent existence, then surely God must be necessary, as between a necessary God and a contingent one, the necessary God meets the criteria of being that than which nothing greater can be conceived.

B. Gaunilo's Response

In Reply on Behalf Of The Fool, Gaunilo responded to both premises of the first version of Anselm's argument, and so sought to undermine its logic.

Version 1 Premise 1: Gaunilo argued that it was possible for a person to understand the definition Anselm gave without committing oneself to accepting its existence or even reality.

Example of the rumour: If I describe a man in full detail, I would use my understanding of 'men' in general to form the image in my mind. But if I were

43

then told that this man did not exist, it would not affect my understanding of the description.

Conclusion: In the same way, I can understand what Anselm means by 'a being than which nothing greater can be conceived' without committing myself to believing it is a real thing.

Version 1 Premise 2: Gaunilo challenged the use of existence as a **PREDICATE**. He argued that one could not simply define God into existence by saying that God's perfection required God to exist.

Example of the island: If I were to describe an island that were perfect in every way, I could well imagine it. But to be told that now by virtue of the fact that I understood it to be perfect, I now must accept it exists in reality, is absurd.

Conclusion: Gaunilo was arguing that that existence **DE DICTO** (by definition) could not lead to existence **DE RE** (in reality). Ultimately, existence is not a predicate and so we cannot list it among God's attributes.

Anselm's Apologetic: Anselm replied to Gaunilo by pointing out that it was impossible to compare God to an island as the island is a **CONTINGENT** thing and God is a **NECESSARY** one. Ultimately, the argument's premises only work for God and for no other thing.

C. Evaluation

Strengths of the Ontological Argument:

1. **Descartes**: Descartes argued in Meditations that existence was a predicate of God in the same way that three sides is a predicate of triangles. Descartes argued that God's nature was perfection and that existence was an attribute of perfection. God's existence needed to be discovered rather than proven.

2. **Alvin Plantinga**: In God, Freedom and Evil supported Anselm in his response to Gaunilo's challenge. Plantinga pointed out that the use of the

island could not possibly undermine the argument as there was no intrinsic maxim that could make an island perfect, since it was a **CONTINGENT** thing. God on the other hand was a necessary being (in theory) and so it is perfectly reasonable to imagine a perfect God. A perfect island is illogical, a perfect God is not.

3. **Charles Hartshorne**: In Anselm's Discovery, he argued that it was true that existence certainly adds something to the properties of a thing. Discussing the symptoms of a sickness could never compare to actually having it. The existence of the sickness adds to the understanding of it and so we can view the existence of God as something more than just the **DE DICTO** definition.

4. **Against Atheism**: The first part of Anselm's argument was to show that the man who says there is no God is a fool. This still applies even if we do not follow Anselm so far as to prove that God must exist necessarily **A PRIORI**. Even the atheist must accept the definition of God, **DE DICTO**, as being the creator of all things. This is a given and does not need to be experienced to be understood. This is what we mean by God. If this is the case, then it is reasonable to postulate that God is not a subject of the universe to be found within the universe. Therefore, it is foolish to think that we can ever "know in our heart" that there is no God as there is no way we could ever prove this.

Weaknesses of the Ontological Argument

1. **Aquinas**: In Summa Theologica, he argued that God is not self-evident to us and, as such, we can never know God's nature. The Ontological Argument assumes that we can know God's nature ourselves. This is impossible.

2. **Immanuel Kant**: In Transcendental Dialectic, he argued that existence could not be a predicate. The statement 'God exists' is of the logical form S is P, that is Subject is Predicate, e.g. Grass is Green. Upon stating that grass is green, we must locate some grass in order to investigate whether or not it is in fact green. Upon finding some we can observe it **A**

POSTERIORI and answer either 'yes' or 'no'. To discover if grass exists we must do the same, find some and then investigate. But upon finding the grass we need look no further at it, as we have shown it exists already. Therefore, existence does not operate like other properties that we need to investigate within a subject. (such as shape or colour). So existence is not a predicate of a subject.

3. **Bertrand Russell**: In Philosophy of Language, he argued that when we talk of the existence of things we talk about X, such that X has some predicates. We search for an X to match these **predicates** and then state 'yes, there is an example' or 'no, there is not'. This is a process of **INSTANTIATION** (providing a specific, real world example of an abstract idea). When we discuss existence we are seeking to instantiate it. We cannot say a thing exists if we cannot instantiate it a posteriori. If we cannot instantiate God, then we can never say "God exists".

Confusion to Avoid

In an essay candidates must always deal with all of Anselm's premises correctly within their respective versions. The challenges of the argument come as challenges to the **PREMISES**. The first that God is in fact a being than which nothing greater can be conceived and that we accept that definition, and the second, that existence is a **PREDICATE**, as existing in reality is better than in the mind alone. To defeat the argument, scholars attack these premises.

Key Quotes

"The fool says in his heart "there is no God"." – Psalm 14:1-3

"There is doubt that there exists a being, than which nothing greater can be conceived, and it exists both in the understanding and in reality." – Anselm

"If a man should try to prove to me by such reasoning that this island truly exists, and that its existence should no longer be doubted, either I should believe that he was jesting, or I know not which I ought to regard as the greater fool." – Gaunilo

"Because we do not know the essence of God, the proposition God exists is not self-evidence to us; but needs to be demonstrated by things that are more known to us." – Aquinas

"All existential propositions are synthetic." – Kant

"To say something exists is to say it is instantiated, or that it actually does appear in existence, not that it is existence is a predicate." – Bertrand Russell

"No matter how great the island is, no matter how many Nubian maidens and dancing girls adorn it, there could always be a greater." – Alvin Plantinga

Suggested Reading

Anselm, Proslogion, Chapter 2-3

Anselm, Apologetic, Chapter 1

St Thomas Aquinas, Summa Theologiciae, 1q q2 a1

Immanuel Kant's Transcendental Dialectic, Book II, Chapter III, Section 4

Practise Exam Question

'Anselm's Ontological Argument proves God exists logically.' Discuss.

AO1 Demonstrate knowledge and understanding through the use of some of the following material. (Maximum 16 marks)

- Outline Anselm's first version of the Ontological Argument, including the definition of God and the painter example.

- Outline Anselm's second version of the Ontological Argument, a clear definition and example of contingent and necessary.

- Outline Gaunilo's response to Anselm's arguments, including the example of the rumour and the example of the island.

AO2 Demonstrate evaluation and analysis through the use of some of the following arguments (maximum 24 marks)

- Explain Gaunilo's challenge that Anselm is moving from de dicto to de re.

- Explain Anselm's response to Gaunilo in his Apologetic.

- Outline contemporary challenges against Anselm's argument, including Kant's S is P challenge and Bertrand Russell's challenge regarding instantiation.

- Outline support for Anselm's argument, including Plantinga's challenge against Gaunilo's Island example and Hartshorne's argument that existence is a predicate.

- Compare the arguments for and against and draw a conclusion.

Possible Future Questions

1. Examine the success of Kant's criticisms to the Ontological Argument.

2. 'Anselm's Ontological Argument proves God exists logically.' Discuss.

3. Assess the claim that existence is a predicate.

4. 'A priori arguments for God's existence are more persuasive than a posteriori arguments.' Discuss

3. God and the World

3.1 Religious Experience

Key Terms

NUMINOUS - The apprehension of the wholly other (a sense of wonder)

RELIGIOUS EXPERIENCE, DIRECT - An encounter with God or an experience received from God (voice, vision, miracle etc)

RELIGIOUS EXPERIENCE, INDIRECT - An understanding about God occurring through some temporal experience (birth, sunset, etc)

PSYCHOLOGICAL NEUROSIS - An experience or way of thinking that is explicitly the product of the mind's functions

Specification

3.1 Religious experience	*3.1.1 The nature and influence of Religious experience*	*A. Examples of mystical religious experiences* *B. Conversion experiences* *C. Conclusions of William James* *D. Evaluation*
	3.1.2 Different ways in which Religious experience can be understood	*A. Union with a great power* *B. Psychological affect* *C. Product of physiological effect* *D. Evaluation*

3.1.1 The Nature And Influence Of Religious Experience

A. Examples of Mystical Religious Experiences

Religious experiences occur throughout history and can be particularly identified within biblical and religious tradition. These experiences have been explored and investigated to discover what makes an experience religious and what, if anything, can qualify it as genuine.

Voice experiences

Voice experiences share these three characteristics:

1. **Disembodied**: The voice will not come directly from a person, but rather will come from heaven or through some inanimate object, e.g. the voice of God came to Moses disembodied through a burning bush (Exodus 3).

2. **Authoritative**: The voice will give a command to the recipient and compel him/her into action based on that experience, e.g. St Paul was compelled to go to Damascus and seek out Ananias to be converted based on the direction of Jesus' voice on the road (Acts of the Apostles 9).

3. **Noetic**: The voice will reveal some knowledge or information to the recipient which they would not have gained any other way, e.g. at Jesus' baptism the voice of God revealed that Jesus was in fact God's Son and that God was pleased with Jesus (Mark 1).

Visions Experiences

Visions fall under one of these three categories:

- **Corporeal**: These visions are of a person in the appearance of flesh and can be interacted with though not everyone will necessarily be about to see them, e.g. St Bernadette saw Mary appear to her as a beautiful woman.

- **Imaginative**: These visions appear within dreams and the recipient may receive particular knowledge or prophecy through it, e.g. Joseph was informed that Mary was pregnant through the power of the Holy Spirit and that he should not be afraid to marry her (Matthew 1).

- **Intellectual**: These visions are more awareness of the presence of some being, being seen with the eye of the mind rather than in physical form, e.g. St Teresa of Avila claims she did not so much see Jesus, but was rather aware of him.

Corporate Religious Experiences

A corporate religious experience is an experience that affects a group of people at the same time. The increased number of witnesses should increase the likelihood of the event as genuine.

- **Pentecost**: The Holy Spirit appeared to the eleven disciple filling them with the gifts of the Holy Spirit and sending them out to preach about Christ.

- **Our Lady of Fatima**: The Virgin Mary appeared to three children in Fatima and encouraged them to pray the rosary for their salvation.

- **The Toronto Blessing**: In Toronto a group of parishioners claimed to be filled with the Holy Spirit, bringing them to hysteria.

B. Conversion experiences

In Varieties of Religious Experiences, William James presented many testimonies of religious experiences, including those of Stephen Bradley and S. H. Hadley. Within the Bible, we see examples of conversions, e.g. the life of St Paul and the change in the life of Moses and various other figures. Within Catholic mystical history we have examples of religious experiences, e.g. from St Bernadette, Teresa of Avila etc. All these experiences share the transient characteristic.

Transience is about long-term effects of an experience. William James argued that the fact that religious experiences have long term effects, e.g. conversions etc. this is evidence that these experiences are genuine. If they were not genuine, they would not have such transient impact on them to make them change their lives and convert to a new way of life.

C. Conclusions of William James

William James argued that religious experiences are **PSYCHOLOGICAL** phenomena; this means that they operate through the psyche. As such all people can have a religious experience; they are not unique to saints.

He argued that Drugs and alcohol can open a recipient up to the divine. In the same way that Indian Yogi train their bodies to be more receptive to the divine, drugs and alcohol can lower the inhibitions of the individual to make them more receptive to the divine without instigating the encounter.

William James identified four characteristics that he identified as common among all forms of religious experiences:

Passive

All religious experiences must happen to the recipient spontaneously in order to be religious; they cannot seek it out, e.g. the persons in the Bible and the mystics of Catholic history did not behave like witchdoctors who entered trances on purpose to receive divine knowledge. They were granted their experiences by God without seeking them out.

Biblical example: Moses was a shepherd in Midian with no intention of returning to Egypt where he was wanted for murder, but experienced an encounter with God regardless in which he was directed to return to Egypt (Exodus 3).

Example in Varieties of Religious Experience: S. H Hadley was sitting alone when he felt a great presence.

Ineffable

All religious experiences must either be beyond human powers to describe or must be of such a nature as they go beyond everyday experiences, so are difficult to grasp and explain.

Biblical example: St Teresa of Avila used creative language to help her describe what she was experiencing and admitted that aspects could not be explained.

Example in Varieties of Religious Experience: Stephen Bradley felt a sense of worthlessness come over him.

Noetic

All religious experiences reveal some knowledge that the recipient could not gain by themselves. This may include the identity of the source of the experience, some theological knowledge or even a deeper understanding of the relationship between God and the recipient.

Biblical example: the angel was told by Mary that she was the Immaculate Conception, a revelation that went on to form Catholic dogma about Mary's nature.

Example in Varieties of Religious Experience: S. H. Hadley came to learn he had experienced Jesus, the sinner's friend.

Transient

While the religious experience is a short encounter, the effects of the experience are long lasting and often involve conversion.

Biblical Example: St Paul was a staunch Jew persecuting the Christians, but following his encounter with Christ he converted to Christianity and became one of the great Apostles of the early Christian Church.

Example in Varieties of Religious Experience: the son of the Oxford Clergyman never touched a drink again after his experience.

D. Evaluation

1. **CHARACTERISTICS** of religious experiences suggested by Richard Swinburne that support William James' characteristics:

- **Public Ordinary**: The interpretation of an ordinary encounter as something spiritual and meaningful, e.g. seeing the earth from orbit and realising how fragile life is.

- **Public Extraordinary**: Being present during a miracle that goes beyond human powers to explain, e.g. witnessing a miraculous healing or one of the biblical miracles.

- **Private Describable**: A Direct religious experience that can be fully described and understood, e.g. the interpretation of one of Joseph's dreams (Genesis 37).

- **Private Non-Describable**: A Direct religious experience which cannot be fully described or understood, e.g. the experiences of St Teresa of Avila.

- **Private Non-Specific**: An Indirect religious experience where the individual sees the world in a different way to help them come to an understanding of God, e.g. Antony Flew's reflection of DNA as proof of God's involvement in the design of the universe.

2. **PRINCIPLES** suggested by Richard Swinburne against which we could verify a religious experience:

- **The Principle of Credulity**: We accept the genuineness of the experiences we have unless we have a compelling reason not to, e.g. we do not believe in God for other reasons, we are drunk etc.

- **The Principle of Testimony**: We should accept the genuineness of other people's testimonies about religious experiences as we accept their testimonies about all other things; there is no difference about a religious experience and so we should not discriminate against religious experiences.

3. **EPISTEMIC IMPERIALISM**: William Alston argued that if we accept our senses with regards to ordinary experiences, there is no reason why we should suddenly stop relying on them in terms of religious experiences. This would be to practice a form of elitism or epistemic imperialism.

4. **MIRACLES** at Lourdes: The Catholic Church has authenticated only 67 of the thousands of miracle claims at **LOURDES**. This authentication comes after decades of investigation by doctors into the claims of the recipients of the apparent miracles. If no other explanation can be found

then the event is declared a miracle and the Church accepts it. If these are in fact miracles, they justify St Bernadette's religious experience as being genuine.

5. **CONSCIOUSNESS** for the Divine: Friedrich Schleiermacher argued that we all have a consciousness for the divine. This supports James' point that religious experiences are natural to us and that we are the ones who block it off by attaching ourselves to the mundane world. From this perspective, **RELIGIOUS EXPERIENCE** is a part of our nature, something that we are naturally designed for.

3.1.2 Different Ways In Which Religious Experience Can Be Understood

A. Union with a great power

Rudolf Otto coined the term '**NUMINOUS**' to describe a religious experience. It means the "apprehension of the wholly other" and was meant to describe how a religious experience was one that is completely apart from anything we can experience in the world. He argued that we need not fully understand a religious experience or be able to explain it, but rather that it only had to relay the Mysterium Tremendum et Fascinans (the awe and mystery) of God.

B. Psychological affect

Sigmund Freud argued that religion was itself a neurosis manifesting childhood experiences and traumas and responding to subconscious fears about the future and death. Belief in God was the **PROJECTION** of the need for an eternal **FATHER FIGURE** and as such had no basis in reality. This being the case, manifest these neurotic ideas into justifications for our behaviour. This is all supported by Freud's research into the obsessive behaviour of patients at Salpêtriére hospital.

56

Timothy Leary conducted experiments where a group of people consumed hallucinogenic drugs and recorded their experiences. These experiences were then compared to the experiences of mystics who claimed to have a religious experience. His findings were that they were indistinguishable from each other. This suggests that there is nothing distinctive about so-called 'religious' experiences. Rather, they are all products of the psyche.

J. L. Mackie argued that if religious experiences were in any way psychological, then those who accept that they have any authority at all are insufficiently critical of them. We should not accept the authority of these experiences if there is any way that they can be accounted for by the psyche itself.

C. Product of physiological effect

Harlow described the character of Phineas Gage, a railway foreman, as agreeable and well-liked. Following the accident which resulted in a pole being thrust into his brain, his character changed markedly. This suggests that any physiological changes to the person that affect the brain in any way, will affect his behaviour and experiences. So, 'religious' experiences can be accounted for by **PHYSIOLOGICAL** changes in the person.

D. Landsborough argued that St Paul may well have suffered temporal lobe epilepsy, which caused his temporary blindness and the voice he heard. The work of Professor Michael Persinger into the effects of magnetism on the temporal lobes supports the theory that if the temporal lobes are affected, then the individual receives what appears to them to be vivid experiences of God or the devil.

Many of the Catholic mystics, St Teresa of Avila, St Bernadette, St Faustina all suffered severe sicknesses prior to their mystical encounters. It is possible that either the sickness or medication they received to combat it instigated the apparent 'religious' experience.

D. Evaluation

Strengths of different ways of interpreting **RELIGIOUS EXPERIENCE**

1. **SEXUAL REPRESSION**: When reading St Teresa of Avila's encounter with the Seraphim from a Freudian perspective, a lot of sexual imagery can be identified. This supports the argument that such experiences are in fact suppressed sexual tension disguised by neurosis and expressed as religious encounters.

2. **OUTDATED VIEW** of the Mind: Modern understanding of the mind has allowed us to probe further into the way we gain knowledge and experiences. This allows us to be more critical about what we experience or think we are experiencing, including 'religious' experiences.

3. **LACK OF RIGOUR**: Anthony O'Hear argued that we should apply checks when considering religious experiences: i. Checking over time; ii. Checking with other senses; iii. Checking with other checkers. If an experience cannot be checked then it is not scientifically verified. While this does not mean that it is not real or genuine, it does mean that we cannot discuss the experience in the same way that we discuss other experiences.

4. **SOCIOLOGICAL SUPPORT**: Karl Marx argued that a person's society directly affects the kinds of experiences they have. A Christian would encounter Jesus or Mary while a Hindu would encounter Vishnu. This is understandable as their societies dictate what they receive. Marx argued that religion was the **OPIUM** of the people. Much like Freud, he was cynical of the role of religion on people's behaviour and so he rejected it. For Marx, the Church was an institution that suppressed the masses so preventing them from flourishing, and so religious experience is part of that institution and propaganda that makes us fall into line. If we believe that God speaks to the leaders of the institution then we are more likely to obey them and do what we are told.

Confusion to Avoid

1. The questions that surround the topic of religious experience all link to one central theme: the **AUTHORITY** of religious experiences over the recipient. If the religious experience is genuine then it has authority over the recipient. If it is not genuine then it should have no authority over them.

2. All challenges to religious experiences are ultimately challenges to the authority we should grant to the experience. If there is a **PSYCHOLOGICAL** influence then the experience is the product of the mind, not the workings of God. If there is a physiological influence, then the experience is the effect of sickness and so we should treat the patient, not deem their words divine. We should always look for the line of debate and see how the question of authority of the experience is probed, and the influence the experience has on the recipient.

3. The **CHARACTERISTICS** of religious experiences do not answer this question by themselves. They should be used in conjunction with the arguments for the genuineness of the experiences and be used to show how religious experiences share characteristics and lead to positive lifestyles and conversions.

Key Quotes

"The sway of alcohol over mankind is unquestionably due to its power to stimulate the mystical faculties of human nature." – William James

"Religion is comparable to a childhood neurosis." – Sigmund Freud

"If it seems to a subject that X is present, then probably X is present; what one seems to perceive is probably so." – Richard Swinburne

Suggested Reading

William James, On Conversion, Lecture IX

William James, On Mysticism, Lecture XVI and XVII

William James, Characteristics of Mystical States of Consciousness, Lectures XVI and XVII

Practise Exam Question

'Religious experiences are nothing more than forms of psychological neurosis.' Discuss.

AO1 Demonstrate knowledge and understanding through the use of some of the following material. (Maximum 16 marks)

- Outline what is meant by a religious experience. Include at least two examples of religious experiences from biblical or religious tradition differentiating between types of religious experiences, e.g. visions and voices.

- Explain why William James considers religious experiences veridical, e.g. the transient impact they have on believers.

- Explain Sigmund Freud's position on religion and religious experiences as a neurosis rather than as a genuine experience.

AO2 Demonstrate evaluation and analysis through the use of some of the following arguments (maximum 24 marks)

- Explore James' view that religious experiences are a psychological phenomenon.

- Support the argument for religious experiences using Richard Swinburne and his principles of Testimony and Credulity.

- Challenge James' argument about religious experiences being psychological with his challenge that they have no authority.

- Support Freud's position using thinkers such as Leary and his critique of mystical accounts and O'Hear's challenge of what makes an experience useable as evidence.

- Compare the arguments and draw a conclusion.

Possible Future Questions

1. 'Corporate religious experiences are less reliable than individual religious experience.' Discuss.

2. Conversion experiences do not provide basis for a belief in God.

3. Assess the claim that religious experiences prove that God exists.

4. Critically compare corporate religious experiences with individual experiences as a basis for belief in God.

3.2 The Problem Of Evil

Key Terms

BENEVOLENCE - The characteristic that God loves us all

MORAL EVIL - The bad things that people do to others to cause suffering

NATURAL EVIL - The bad things that happen in nature that cause suffering

OMNIPOTENCE - The belief that God has all power to do anything

OMNISCIENCE - The belief that God knows all that is happening in the world

Specification

3.2 The Problem of Evil	3.2.1 Different Presentations of the Problem of Evil and Suffering	A. Logical Aspects of the Problem B. Evidential Aspects of the Problem
	3.2.3 Theodicies	A. Augustine's Theodicy B. Hick's Theodicy C. Evaluation

3.2.1 The Problem Of Evil And Suffering

The Problem of Evil and Suffering, named the "rock of atheism" by Hans Kung, challenges the belief in God based on the classical Judaeo-Christian understanding that God is **BENEVOLENT**, all-powerful and all-knowing. The revealed nature of God is incompatible with the existence of evil and suffering in the world, and so this inconsistency proves that there can be no God.

A. Logical Aspects of the Problem

i. The Inconsistent Triad

This is the classical challenge against God's existence based in two key attributes assigned to God and the existence of evil and suffering in the world. It was originally used by Epicurus, but David Hume also presented it:

Is God able to prevent evil, but not able? Then he is not omnipotent. Is God able, but not willing? Then he is **MALEVOLENT**. Is he both able and willing? Then where does evil come from? Is he neither able nor willing? Then why call him God?

This argument identifies evil with suffering and suggests that if God did exist and were God an all loving, all powerful God as He is presented in classical Christian Theology, then God would both want and be able to prevent suffering amongst human beings whom he created and supposedly loves. The fact that suffering persists is indication that there is not a loving God who sustains and watches over the world otherwise He would do something to relieve that suffering.

ii. C. J.L. Mackie and H.L. McCloskey's Logical Problem of Evil

Mackie and McCloskey presented a variation to the classical Inconsistent Triad by including God's supposed **OMNISCIENCE** to the equation.

1. God is **OMNIPOTENT**. He is able to stop evil.

2. God is **OMNISCIENT**. He knows about the suffering that would happen.

3. God is **OMNIBENEVOLENT**. He does not want us to suffer.

4. Evil exists. People suffer though God knows about it, can and wants to prevent it.

This variation places the moral accountability on God as, not only should God want and be able to prevent suffering, God intentionally created a world where He knew suffering would take place. God directly and willingly created a world where He knew people would suffer and die. This pre-knowledge shows that there cannot be a good and powerful God.

B. Evidential Aspects of the Problem

i. John Stuart Mill's Evil Nature

Mill argued that the evil and suffering within the natural world is enough to prove that there can be no **BENEVOLENT** designer of the world as no good being would permit such suffering within nature.

Richard Dawkins used the **DIGGER WASP** to develop this point. The wasp paralyses the caterpillar to lay eggs inside it. When the eggs hatch, the caterpillar suffers and dies. This shows evil in nature.

ii. Natural and Moral Evils

Peter Vardy identified five types of natural suffering that takes place in the world.

1. Natural disasters: earthquakes, tsunamis etc.

2. Diseases: cancer, diabetes etc.

3. Psychological illness: bipolar, multiple personality, autism etc.

4. Human frailty: pain during childbirth, colds and susceptibility to sickness.

5. Animal suffering: animals being killed by other animals.

Brian Hebblethwaite argued that moral evil, the evils done to others, is received and experienced by our naturally occurred senses. For this reason, moral evils are in fact naturally suffered and so moral evil is also a type of natural evil.

3.2.2 The Theodicies

A. Augustine's Theodicy

St Augustine argued that evil and suffering were not accountable to God, but rather to humanity. His theodicy was an attempt to demonstrate how we are ultimately responsible for the evil and suffering in the world.

1. **EVIL IS A PRIVATION**: Augustine said that evil did not exist as a thing in itself but rather was a lack of something. God created all things perfectly and evil is only a corruption of that good thing. In the same way that bad teeth are simply good teeth that have not been taken care of, evil in the world is good things that have not been nurtured and cared

for, people not doing what they are supposed to be doing. So all that is evil came from God but when it did, it was still good.

2. **READING OF GENESIS**: Augustine was not a **CREATIONIST** and so did not believe in the literal interpretation of Genesis 1 and 2, however, he used it to help teach how evil entered the world. It is through human disobedience that evil comes into the world.

3. **NATURAL EVIL**: Augustine appealed to the Creation story in Genesis to explain how natural evil entered God's otherwise perfect world. Augustine believed that the Fall of Mankind means that suffering is a punishment for sin. He also believed that the fall of some angels (given too little grace) meant that the fabric of universe was disordered, which brings about natural suffering.

4. **THE ESCHATOLOGICAL QUESTION**: In the end (**ESCHATON** = the end-times) God will judge us all based on our actions and how much we obeyed or disobeyed God.

B. Hick's Theodicy

John Hick's theodicy was heavily influenced by Irenaeus' theodicy, written 2nd Century.

i. Irenaeus' Theodicy

1. **SUFFERING IS GOOD**: Primarily, Irenaeus argued that suffering was not in itself a bad thing, but rather a **NECESSARY TOOL** to help us develop as human beings. We need suffering, risk and pain in order to make the right choices and develop as people. If we live a life without suffering we will never learn anything and will never value the **GOODNESS OF GOD**.

2. **READING GENESIS**: While Irenaeus was a **CREATIONIST**, he did not see it necessary to read Genesis in that way in order to learn from it. He argued that the example of Adam and Eve was just the first time human

beings disobey God and are punished for it. We disobey God all the time and are punished and it is always the tempter who receives the greater punishment. However, Adam and Eve, in their infancy, could not have really been expected to know right from wrong, and so we can take comfort from that. God's punishment was a just punishment and it led to them learning and developing as it does for us.

3. **IMAGE AND LIKENESS**: Irenaeus' theodicy requires us to re-read the creation story slightly. While God created us in his **IMAGE**, in that we are capable of rational and moral thinking, He did not create us in his **LIKENESS,** but rather we need to live, learn and suffer in order to gain God's likeness.

ii. Hick's Variation of Irenaeus' Theodicy

1. **SOUL-MAKING**: John Hick took Irenaeus' theodicy and developed it in order to make sense of it in a modern world. He argued that we are on earth for the purpose of **SOUL-MAKING**. That is, we need to learn and grow on earth and make our souls more like God. This happens through suffering. For this reason, Christians see suffering as sometimes a good thing as it allows us to share Christ's suffering and make us more like Him.

2. **EPISTEMIC DISTANCE**: We are created at a distance from God, not a geographical distance (e.g. land and sky), but rather an **EPISTEMIC** one (episteme is Greek for knowledge), a **KNOWLEDGE GAP** that cannot be crossed on our terms. God has set this distance so humanity has awareness of God but not certainty. Humans are not born with the **INNATE KNOWLEDGE** of God's existence and have to seek God through faith. Through our lives we must work on our souls in order to make them more perfect so that we can cross that distance. However, that can never be perfectly done in a lifetime, so eschatologically (at the end of time) God will cover that distance for us. This leads to the (possibly unchristian) belief in universal salvation that in the end all will be saved.

3. **CHRIST, THE NEW ADAM**: Hick argued that Christ was the **NEW ADAM** and did what Adam could not do, resist temptation and ultimately show us how to be perfect. In fact, Christ tells us in Matthew to "be perfect, as your Father in heaven is perfect". This is our call and while we are not perfect on earth we suffer through **NATURAL** and **MORAL** evil as Christ suffered before us. However, through baptism we are working our souls to become more like Christ and be saved.

C. Evaluation

Strengths of Augustine's Theodicy

1. **BRIAN DAVIES**: Brian Davies supported Augustine's notion that evil is a **PRIVATION** rather than a substance in his example of bad deckchairs and sour grapes, all of which were examples of fallen objects. In fact, this model of good and evil marries directly with Aristotle's notion of goodness being the fulfilment of ones' final cause. If one does not, they are bad, if they cannot then they are corrupt.

2. **ALVIN PLANTINGA**: Alvin Plantinga argued in The Free Will Defence that Augustine was right that moral evil is accountable to human beings and that we cannot blame God, as it is better that God created free agents than obedient robots and where there is freedom there must be the freedom to disobey God.

Strengths of Hick's Theodicy

1. **NO PROBLEM**: This theodicy avoids the problems of a **PERFECT CREATION** going wrong which Augustine's theodicy faces. Since evil is part of God's creation there is no "problem of evil" as such, as evil is part of "the plan of God".

2. **DEVELOPMENT**: This theodicy explains the importance of life on earth as a time of **DEVELOPMENT** and spiritual growth. This is absent in other theodicies and explains why we are here at all.

3. **BEST OF ALL POSSIBLE WORLDS**: Gottfried Leibniz argued that this must be the best of all possible worlds and Hick's theodicy follows that model in that this is the only way the world could be. Without freedom we would be incapable of **GOODNESS** and without suffering we would be incapable of **GROWTH**.

Weaknesses of Augustine's Theodicy

1. **LOGICAL CONTRADICTION**: **SCHLEIERMACHER** pointed out the in the idea that God created a perfect world, which went wrong. Augustine did not address this. Grapes can go sour if you leave them out in the sun, but why would God leave us to go wrong – surely God's perfect nature would inform him of what will go wrong and he would address it?

2. **INTERPRETING GENESIS**: Since **AUGUSTINE** did not believe in the **LITERAL INTERPRETATION** of the Creation story or the story of the Fall of Adam, it makes no sense for him to rely on it so heavily in order to explain **NATURAL EVIL** in the world. The idea that all natural evil comes from the fallen angels who rebelled following the Fall of Adam seems far-fetched and inadequate to explain what we experience as tectonic plate movement (earthquake) and the various other types of natural evil that Peter Vardy identifies.

3. **HELL**: The existence of **HELL** suggests that God knew his creation would disobey Him and that things would go 'wrong'. If God knew they would go this way, is it wrong? If not, and it was intended, then surely that justifies **IRENAEUS**' theodicy.

Weaknesses of Hick's Theodicy

1. **UNIVERSAL SALVATION**: Hick's theodicy requires an **UNORTHODOX** reading of creation, in that we are meant to believe we are not made in God's image and likeness, which the Catholic Church maintains we are. Further, the principle of **UNIVERSAL SALVATION**, which Hick argues, is again counter to mainstream Christianity. The belief that we might go to hell if we are bad is a necessity if God is good and

just and we are free. If we are all destined to go to heaven no matter what we do then there is no need to be 'good' on earth at all.

2. **UNFAIR**: This theodicy argues that we have suffering in order to learn and make our souls complete, but this does not justify the deaths of infants and even the unborn that had no chance to live or learn. Their deaths cannot help them to grow or make their souls. In fact, those who do evil to others often live longer than their victims, and so how are they learning?

3. **END JUSTIFYING THE MEANS**: The **END** cannot morally justify the **MEANS**. Even if evil and suffering (the **MEANS**) did enable us to forge perfect souls (the **END**, there is so much evil and suffering that surely God would be able to find another way, e.g. a life simulator where people did not actually suffer.

Confusion to Avoid

1. St Augustine uses the **FALL** of Adam and Eve to explain human **FREE WILL** and wickedness. In fact, he argued that **ORIGINAL SIN** alone was enough to damn all humanity to hell. However, Augustine was not a Creationist; he did not believe that the Creation stories of Genesis were intended to be literally read. Conversely, St Irenaeus' theodicy teaches it does not matter if Adam and Eve were real, as every time we disobey God we are repeating the sin of Adam and Eve, but he was in fact a **CREATIONIST**.

Key Quotes

"Evil comes from God'. It was obvious to me that things which are liable to corruption are good. If there were no good in them there would be nothing capable of being corrupted.' – St Augustine

"When a thing is corrupted, its corruption is an evil because it is a privation of the good." – St Augustine

"Nearly all the things which men are hanged or imprisoned for doing to one another are nature's everyday performances." – John Stuart Mill

"Humanity is created at an epistemic distance from God in order to come freely to know and love their Maker; and that they are at the same time created." – John Hick

Suggested Reading

St Augustine, City of God, Book 9 Chapter 9

St Augustine, City of God, Book 12 Chapter 6

St Augustine, Confessions, Book 7 Chapter 3

St Augustine, Confessions, Book 7 Chapter 5 and 7

Mackie and McCloskey, Logical Problem of Evil, Part 1

Practise Exam Question

Critically assess whether it is possible to defend monotheism in the face of the existence of evil.

AO1 Demonstrate knowledge and understanding through the use of some of the following material. (Maximum 16 marks)

- Outline the Problem of Evil and Suffering, including aspects of the logical and evidential problems of evil.

- Explain how the problem of evil and suffering challenges the classical view of the monotheistic God as being all loving, all powerful and all knowing.

- Outline Augustine's theodicy. Explain Augustine's view of privation and outline his view of natural evil as a consequence of the fall of humanity and the angels.

- Outline Hick's theodicy. Explain the issue of soul making and outline the notion of being created at an epistemic distance from God.

- Explain how Augustine's and Hick's theodicies seek to resolve the challenges raised by the Problem of Evil and Suffering.

AO2 Demonstrate evaluation and analysis through the use of some of the following arguments (maximum 24 marks)

- Identify the strengths and weaknesses of Augustine's theodicy, including the problems raised by his view of origin of natural suffering.

- Identify the strengths and weaknesses of Hick's theodicy, including the problems raised by God's knowledge of the suffering of innocent human beings.

- Evaluate the problem of evil and suffering and whether or not it really proves the lack of existence of God or whether suffering can work within a monotheistic worldview.

- Compare the positions and draw a conclusion

Possible Future Questions

1. Critically compare the logical and evidential aspects of the problem of evil as challenges to belief.

2. Assess the claim that natural evil has a purpose.

3. Critically discuss the theodicy of Augustine.

4. 'There is no solution to the problem of evil and suffering.' Discuss.

4. Nature of God

Key Terms

BENEVOLENT – The belief that God is all loving.

ETERNAL – The belief that God exists not inside time, but outside it. God is a-temporal.

EVERLASTING – On-going within the universe.

PREDESTINATION – the belief that God has already decided what will happen to you.

OMNIPOTENCE – The belief that God is all-powerful.

OMNISCIENCE – The belief that God is all-knowing.

TIMELESS – The belief that God is outside of time.

Specification

4. Nature of God	4.1 Omnipotent	A. Evidence B. Interpretation
	4.2 Benevolent	A. Hell B. Judgement
	4.3 Omniscient	A. Unlimited B. Limited
	4.4 Eternal	A. Timeless B. Four Dimentionalist C. Everlasting
	4.5 Free Will	A. Boethius' dilemma B. Alternative responses

4.1 Omnipotence

A. Evidence

1. Biblical revelation

In Genesis we see a great deal of evidence to suggest that God is **OMNIPOTENT**, in various examples of theophany, e.g. the Creation story, the Flood and the miracles God performs. The Creation story lends to the Judeo-Christian tradition belief that God created the world ex nihilo –from nothing.

- With only the power of his commands, all things come to be.
- The story of the Flood shows the worldly consequences when God chooses to remove his sustaining hand.

- Finally, in the various examples of miracles within the Bible, not least when He stops the sun in the sky to give Joshua time to defeat the Amorites in the Book of Joshua, show that God can act in the world and does so with great limitless power.

2. Greek Philosophical Thought

The Essential **FORM** of Goodness, theorised by **PLATO** in his Republic, was later identified with Plotinus' The One, the God that is responsible for all things. In this way, God can be identified with what Plato took to be the Essential **FORM** of Goodness which gives life to all things, and in this way, God is all powerful as He is the source of all that is.

Further, in **ARISTOTLE**'s Metaphysics, we see the nature of the Prime Mover, that which draws all things to itself, the telos of the world; the first motion that moves all other things in the universe. Such is the power of God.

B. Interpretations

1. God's ability to do anything including the logically impossible.

The attitude that God can do the logically possible and impossible appears in the work of the French mathematician Rene Descartes. God created the universe and so all apparent logic within it is part of that creation including the axioms which are the foundation of all rational knowledge. Since it is all part of God's creation, God is above maths and logic and so God cannot be bound by or subject to it. Therefore, if he wished to change it, He has the power to do so. God is not limited by our understanding of what is logically possible.

Pete Vardy argued that God does not do anything He wants because he places a **SELF-LIMITATION** on his power. God chooses how to use his power and when not to use it. For this reason, God does not stop suffering or reveal himself directly. God chooses how to limit his own power.

2. God's ability to do what is logically possible for God to do.

This attitude is notably held by St Thomas Aquinas. Certain limitations can be placed upon what God can do, including: changing history, sinning, being caught in logical traps, e.g. climbing trees or creating square circles etc. Aquinas's notion of God's omnipotence only took into account what logic would permit. Anything that contradicts itself cannot be considered part of God's **OMNIPOTENCE**, e.g. if by square we mean four-sided shape, it is logically contradictory to expect God to create a one-sided four-sided shape. That is a limitation of our own understanding, not of God. If we accept history as events that have happened, we cannot logically expect God to make events that have happened not have happened. That is a limitation on our understanding, not God's power.

3. Omnipotence is a statement of the power of God.

Taking the Bible as the primary source of our understanding of God of Judeo-Christian tradition being omnipotent, we can read revelation about omnipotence in one of two ways: propositionally and non-propositionally.

- **PROPOSITIONAL** reading: If we read the Bible propositionally, we must accept all propositions about God's power as statements of fact. The problem is that statements like 'God held the sun in the sky' give us varied and inexplicable gauges for God's power.

- **NON-PROPOSITIONAL** reading: If we read the Bible non-propositionally, then statements like 'God made the world in six days' have a symbolic meaning and are reflections of people's understanding about God, not qualifications of what God's **OMNIPOTENCE** means. The problem is that we do not accurately know what it means to call God **OMNIPOTENT** at all.

4.2 Benevolence

A. Hell

Challenge: How can a **BENEVOLENT** God allow anyone to go to hell?

Answer: The Roman Catholic Church encourages the acceptance of belief in Saints who are in heaven, but has never committed itself to stating that anyone is in hell as only God can judge the heart. Ultimately, God does not want people to go to hell, however, if God is love and if humans have free will, then that love must be all encompassing and any human freedom that seeks to reject it must lovingly be accepted. Therefore, God is bound by his own nature to allow for hell, the place where people send themselves through their own rejection of God's love. Another way of thinking about hell is as C. S. **LEWIS** said: *'the door to hell is locked from the inside'*. This means that it is we who choose to condemn ourselves, not God who wishes to condemn us.

B. Judgement

Challenge: **BOETHIUS** questioned how God could fairly reward and punish, particularly if we did not have free will to decide our own actions.

Answer: Boethius resolved, through the voice of **LADY PHILOSOPHY**, that God's perspective of time is completely different to ours. God has the peculiar ability to see every human being's action in the present of his or her action. Alongside God's eternal nature, God can see all human action without interfering with it. Therefore, God can see all human action across time as though an observer and so God alone can judge human actions as human actions are free under the gaze of God's infallible Providence. This fairness and judgement is part of God's **BENEVOLENCE**.

4.3 Omniscience

A. Unlimited Knowledge

BOETHIUS presented the argument, through the voice of Lady Philosophy, that God's omniscience is unlimited. God's knows all things because of the peculiar nature of God. God knows the past, present and the future, because all time is present to God and so God has all knowledge of all time.

AQUINAS echoed this view by arguing that knowledge is immaterial, so God, who is immaterial, can possess knowledge. There is nothing that God cannot know. As God reveals to Job in scripture, God himself put the stars in the sky and built the foundations of the earth, so God alone knows all things. Any decision is known to God and nothing can fool Him.

B. Limited Knowledge

Richard **SWINBURNE** had difficulty accepting the idea that God had all knowledge as, in his reading, it did not fit with scripture where God appears to respond to human actions in the world. Additionally, he considered there to be a conflict between unlimited knowledge and human free will. God's knowledge is in fact limited as God only knows the present and the past. God cannot know the future so there can be no question of God knowing our actions before they happen, nor of accountability for any evil and suffering that takes place, as God is not aware of it.

We see evidence of this in **GENESIS** and in **1 SAMUEL** where God learns that Adam and Eve have disobeyed Him and where he is displeased with David's decisions after they have all taken place.

4.4 Eternity

A. Timeless

i. Boethius

As part of Boethius's solution to the conflict between God's omniscience and human free will, Boethius, through the voice of Lady Philosophy, sought to show that God's nature was eternal. By this, Boethius meant that God did not exist within the world but completely apart from it. This echoes Augustine who said that God had to be **TRANSCENDENT** otherwise God could not have been the creator of the world.

He gives the example of the man watching another man sitting. One places a necessity on the other. 'A' must be sitting if 'B' sees 'A' sitting. And 'B' must be watching 'A' sitting if 'A' is actually sitting. So if God sees beforehand what I do, then He necessitates it. Lady Philosophy resolves this problem by identifying God's perspective as one of an **ETERNAL** God outside time.

Lady philosophy suggested the problem was in human understanding of **ETERNITY**, rather than the problem of God's knowledge. Knowledge is dependent not on the subject, but the knower. In the same way that an adult can know a phone in a more sophisticated way to a baby, God can know us in a more sophisticated way than we know each other. She presented four spheres of knowledge: 1. Sensory, 2. Imaginative, 3. Rational, 4. Pure Intellectual. A knower of one sphere can know the previous but never the next so we can never know subjects as God knows them. Additionally, Lady Philosophy suggested that God's **ETERNAL** perspective means that He sees every event in history in a perfect present, not in temporal sequence but in an **A-TEMPORAL PRESENT**. So time does not pass for God, it is static. We experience time, God does not. In this way, God can know all things without influencing them for human beings.

ii. Augustine and Aquinas

AUGUSTINE discusses the problem of considering a 'time' before God since it was God who created time. Augustine sees God's as transcendent, that is a-temporal and outside of space itself. So God's **ETERNITY** means that God is timeless. All questions of God's nature must be considered from a non-spatiotemporal perspective. If God is outside of time, then God cannot change as change requires time. God is immutable which suggests that God wills from **ETERNITY**. There was never a time when God changed what he wills. E.g. God must have willed the universe **ETERNALLY**.

This position was later reaffirmed by Aquinas who was heavily influenced by Boethius and Augustine. He repeats Boethius notion that God sees everything in an **ETERNAL** simultaneous present. Aquinas sees God as the unmoved mover, uncaused cause. This can only make sense if God is an **ETERNAL TRANSCENDENT** being. From this position, God is timeless.

Anthony **KENNY** criticises Aquinas with his challenge that if his own writings are simultaneous with **ETERNITY** as is Rome's burning under Nero, then the writing of Kenny's paper takes place simultaneously as Nero's actions. This is a misunderstanding. God sees all simultaneously, this does not mean that two temporal events are simultaneous with each other. All temporal events follow the course of time, but God observes them simultaneously because of the peculiar nature of God being **TIMELESS**.

B. Four Dimentionalist Approach

ANSELM presented another approach called the four-dimentionalist approach. It was a variation of Boethius' view that God exists timelessly; however, rather than placing God outside of time, Anselm placed God within all times - omni-present, in all times, all of the time. God is everywhere in every time and in every place, so God knows everything because God is everywhere. But God does not force action, because God is present everywhere in an **OBSERVATIONAL** sense, not a controlling sense.

Where Boethius and Aquinas describe God as seeing he whole road as though from a mountaintop, for Anselm, God is at every point along the road, the start, middle and end, completely immersed in the world.

C. Everlasting

This position is presented by Richard Swinburne as part of his attempt to reconcile God's **OMNISCIENCE** with the problem of evil and suffering and free will. Within the Bible, God is revealed to learn along the same timeline as we do. God learns as we learn. This can only make sense if God is **EVERLASTING** within the universe rather than outside of it. Swinburne argued that for God to know what it is to be in the world in 1995, He needed to be in the world in 1995. This perspective also makes sense in terms of how we build a relationship with God. If God is within the world, then we can pray to God and He can answer. God can perform miracles and take an interest in our lives. If God is **ETERNAL**, then, as Boethius suggests, prayers are in vain as God cannot respond to them as God is immutable.

Swinburne's position does have weaknesses. As Augustine suggested, if God created all things then time is one of those things and God cannot be subject to time. Additionally, this limits God considerably as God is now subject to time. It raises questions about how God could create the world if God is within the boundaries of the world and time.

4.5 Free Will

A. Boethius' Dilemma

In Consolations of Philosophy, Boethius presents his dilemma of how he can be free if God has all knowledge. He gives the example of one man sitting and another man watching. In this example, he suggests that the action (the man sitting) places **NECESSITY** on the observation (the other man watching). But in turn, the truth of the observation necessitates the reality of the action. When the action comes first, there is no problem, but when the observation comes first (as with Providence), this destroys free will as human actions are necessitated by God's knowledge of them.

Through the voice of **LADY PHILOSOPHY**, Boethius resolves that in fact God's Providence exists eternally and so knows everything in its own present rather than in time before they happen. Providence looks forth rather than forward as though from a mountaintop. For this reason, Providence's Omniscient perspective does not interfere with human free will in any way, and so humans are free to act and pray to God.

B. Alternative Responses

1. **SCHLEIERMACHER** attempts to resolve the problem by suggesting that God's knowledge is like that of friends, intimate and accurate by not controlling.

2. **LUIS OF MOLINA** attempted to explain it by suggesting that God knows all possible futures, but Elizabeth Anscombe argued that such knowledge would be no knowledge at all.

3. Additionally, Gottfried **LEIBNIZ** argued that this was the best of all possible worlds, so there would be no alternative futures for God to know.

Confusions to Avoid

1. If the exam question asks about omnipotence, use the knowledge on God's omnipotence. However, if the question asks about benevolence, omniscience, eternity or free will, these all work together. Ensure you are referring to Boethius in answering this style of question.

2. The problem of evil is indeed a problem raised by each of the characteristics of God: **OMNIPOTENCE**, **BENEVOLENCE**, **OMNISCIENCE** and **ETERNITY**. However, any questions in this section will not be expecting a Problem of Evil essay. Rather, the problems can be raised but should be raised directly with regard to the

nature of that characteristic, and solutions should be presented that are in line with addressing that characteristic.

Key Quotes

'In the Beginning…God said "Let there be light" and there was light.' – Genesis 1

'God said: "Let there be light", and there was light.' – Genesis 1:4

"With God, all things are possible." – Mark 10:27

'Without Him, nothing was made that is made.' – John 1:3

"For God to sin would mean losing control of his actions which is illogical as it would mean he is not be omnipotent." – St Anselm

"You have made all times, and you are before all times, and not at any time was there no time." – Augustine

"Whatever involves a contradiction is not held by omnipotence, for it just cannot possibly make sense of being possible." – St Thomas Aquinas

"God's power can do anything." – St Thomas Aquinas

"Eternity is simultaneously whole while time is not, eternity measuring abiding existence, time measuring change." – St Thomas Aquinas

"God can do anything, including what might seem impossible." – Rene Descartes

"I do not think that we should ever say of anything that it cannot be brought about by God." – Rene Descartes

"You can't say God knows the events of AD 1995 unless it means that he exists in 1995 and knows in 1995 what is happening." – Richard Swinburne

Suggested Reading

Anselm, Proslogion, Chapter 2

Boethius, Consolations of Philosophy, Book 5

Richard Swinburne, The Coherence of Theism, 12 Eternal and Immutable

Peter Vardy, The Puzzle of Evil, Chapter 15 The Challenge of Freedom

Practise Exam Question

Evaluate the philosophical problems raised by the belief that God is eternal.

AO1 Demonstrate knowledge and understanding through the use of some of the following material. (Maximum 16 marks)

- Explain how an eternal God would have unlimited omniscience and how this causes conflict with human free will, as shown by Boethius.

- Explain how a timeless God that did not have unlimited omniscience would not be the God of classical theism.

- Explain how an everlasting God would resolve the conflict raised by omniscience and free will as shown by Swinburne but would conflict with the God of classical theism.

AO2 Demonstrate evaluation and analysis through the use of some of the following arguments (maximum 24 marks)

- Outline the two possible definitions of what is meant by eternal: Timeless and Everlasting.

- Present Lady Philosophy's argument that God's eternity is a simultaneous possession of infinite life. Support this with Augustine and Aquinas.

- Explain how Lady Philosophy's understanding of God's eternity resolves the conflict between omniscience and free will.

Possible Future Questions

1. Assess Boethius' view that divine eternity does not limit human free will.

2. Critically assess the philosophical problems raised by believing in an omnibenevolent God.

3. Assess the claim that the universe shows no evidence of the existence of a benevolent God.

4. Critically assess the problems for believers who say that God is omniscient.

5. Boethius was successful in his argument that God rewards and punishes justly. Discuss.

6. Critically assess the philosophical problems raised by belief that God is omniscient.

5. Classical Religious Language

Key Terms

ANALOGY – Comparing two things, by knowing the one we can understand the other.

APOPHATIC WAY – The Via Negativa.

ATTRIBUTION – The attributes of one reveal the attributes of the other.

CATAPHATIC WAY – The Via Positiva.

EQUIVOCAL – The same word has a different meaning when applied to two things.

PROPORTION – Things are proportionate to their own natures.

SIGN –Arbitrary indicator of something else. Useful as long as we agree on what it means.

SYMBOL – When a term is linked to the subject to which it refers.

UNIVOCAL – A word has the same literal meaning when applied to two things.

VIA NEGATIVA – The belief that the only way to talk about God is with negative language.

VIA POSITIVA – The belief that you can talk meaningfully about God with positive language.

Specification

5. Classical Religious Language	5.1 Apophatic Way	A. Speaking with certainty B. Moses Maimonides C. Teresa of Avila D. Evaluation
	5.2 Cataphatic Way	A. The need for analogy B. Analogy of Attribution C. Analogy of Proportionality D. Evaluation
	5.3 Symbolism	A. What are signs and symbols? B. Paul Tillich on signs and symbols C. Use of Symbols in scripture and religious language D. Evaluation

5.1 The Apophatic Way

A. Speaking with Certainty

The **APOPHATIC WAY** is an approach to Religious Language that suggests we can only talk about God using negative language. Without realising it, we use **VIA NEGATIVA** all the time when discussing God. Terms like immortal, immaterial, immutable, immanent etc. are all **VIA NEGATIVA** terms which emphasise the point that God is apart from this universe, beyond all human comprehension and understanding.

For example, Plato's Essential FORM of Goodness was an abstract notion, not in time or space, and so it is impossible to say anything about it except that it is what gives life to all things and is the source of all goodness. But there is nothing to say about it directly. Plotinus, the Neo Plotinus, identified the Essential FORM of Goodness with God, and so God takes on that abstraction.

BOETHIUS, **AUGUSTINE** and Thomas **AQUINAS** all argued that God existed in a timeless eternity. This being the case, we prove that He exists or does not exist. He is, as John **HICK** terms it, at an epistemic distance from us. As shown in the study of Religious Experience, any direct revelation of God is ineffable to us. Since our language is rooted in our human experiences and God is beyond all human experiences, no language can adequately describe any aspect of God's nature. Therefore, we cannot ever speak with any certainty about God.

B. Moses Maimonides

In his work, Guide to the Perplexed, Moses **MAIMONIDES** reminded his putative readers that there was no need to ever use **POSITIVE LANGUAGE** to try to glorify God.

i. God can better be understood through negation.

Moses Maimonides gave an interesting example of how negation can accurately lead one to understanding a subject without any recourse to **POSITIVE LANGUAGE**. The example was of a ship and the method of emphasising the superiority of the **VIA NEGATIVA** was to play a form of 20 questions where, by process of elimination, a group of enquirers would eventually come to understand that the subject in question – a ship – as it was not a mineral, a solid, a sphere etc.

ii. Any attempt to use positive language would ultimately lead to loss of faith.

Maimonides' additional point has some merit to it. Consider the notions of Sigmund **FREUD** (obviously Maimonides did not consider Freud as Freud lived 700 years after Maimonides), that we project our desire for an eternal father figure to create the idea of God. By using **POSITIVE LANGUAGE** to describe God, we are using the language of human experience, and in doing so, we are projecting our human desires onto an external figure. Indirectly, we are reducing God to a human construct and assigning anthropomorphic characteristics to Him. These characteristics would then be contradictory. Take for example the quality of omnipotence. As previously shown, by seeing God's omnipotence as the ability to do anything as we understand it, we fall into problems: what it means, how we deal with suffering etc. In this way, we find ourselves doubting God's existence, all because we used positive language.

C. Teresa of Avila

TERESA OF AVILA was a 16th Century Spanish mystic who received many religious experiences and recorded them. In her writings she clearly shows the ineffability of God as revealed to her. Ineffability literally means that something cannot be explained or defined. While not all Teresa of Avila's writings are in the form of **VIA NEGATIVA** (e.g. the description of the angel with the golden lance), we can interpret that she used figurative language to account for experiences which were in themselves beyond ordinary human experience (e.g. 'he left me aflame with love for God').

Teresa of Avila often describes the **INEFFABILITY** of her experience when she states that she does not in fact see Christ, '*I told him that I did not know how I knew it was the Christ, but that I could not help realising that He was beside me.*' This clear lack of clarity in her description shows that her experience is not corporeal or imaginative but rather is intellectual. This denotes that the experience is not ordinary, and that Teresa of Avila has borrowed language from human experience to help mediate its meaning.

The **VIA NEGATIVA** emphasises the ineffability of God's nature. He goes beyond all human powers to understand and describe. The fact that we must resort to **NEGATIVE LANGUAGE** shows that God goes beyond all comprehension.

D. Evaluation

Strengths of the Apophatic Way

1. **GOD'S NATURE**: The Via Negativa identifies that God's nature goes beyond the experiences of everyday life. This can be linked back to Plato's description of the Essential FORM of Goodness.

2. **EPISTEMIC DISTANCE**: Since God is at an epistemic distance from us, any positive human language fails to accurately describe God. God is essentially other, as Pseudo-Dionysius describes.

3. **LOSS OF FAITH**: In attempting to positively describe God we will ultimately lose our fail in God as we reduce Him to a human construct.

Weaknesses of the Apophatic Way

1. **SHIP EXAMPLE**: As Moses Maimonides' example of the ship ironically shows, if God is beyond our understanding, no process of elimination will ever reach Him and so we can learn nothing about God using Via

Negativa. As Brian Davies commented that the subject could quite easily be a wardrobe as a ship, such was the limited power of the process of elimination. Further, unless the subject is already in the understanding of the audience, the process of elimination will never result in reaching the subject. If God is outside human experience and all I have to go in is my experience, I will never reach the understanding of God.

2. **UNFALSIFIABLE**: By describing God through negation, we are in fact doing little more than refuting any qualities and refusing to qualify anything to Him. This causes the un-falsifiability problems raised by Anthony Flew.

3. **SCRIPTURE**: We see positive language used to describe God in scripture and within communities of fail. In Christianity, God is described as Father. This is a positive description.

4. **RELIGIOUS LANGUAGE IS ABOUT A RELATIONSHIP WITH GOD**: When we speak about God, we are saying actual things about Him, and building a relationship.

5.2 The Cataphatic Way

A. The need for Analogy

Aquinas considered how religious language is actually used by believers as a means to communicate about God and build a relationship with Him. While he began his career as a user of **VIA NEGATVIA**, he finally rejected it famously describing how calling God 'the Living God' we are saying more than 'God is not dead'.

Typically, language is either **UNIVOCAL** or **EQUIVOCAL**. **UNIVOCAL** language is when a term is used in the same way in two different situations: where I say 'the oven is hot' and 'the desert is hot', I mean 'hot' in the same way. Whereas, **EQUIVOCAL** language is the use of the same word but meaning different things, for example, 'I am scared of bats' and 'cricket uses bats'; we mean two different things here. Aquinas suggested that **ANALOGY** was an alternative approach to language where we can use language properly but mean different things due to the nature of that which we are discussing.

B. Analogy of Attribution

Aquinas said that the relationship between two things was the basis for an **ANALOGY**. He gave the example of the urine and the medicine. If a physician were to prescribe medicine and, following its correct use, the patient's urine were to improve, this would indicate that the medicine was working. While being completely different, the qualities of the first (the medicine) lead to the qualities of the second (the urine). In this way, we can attribute the qualities of the second to the first. By doing this, we can speak about God using our language and understanding about the world.

This example was supported by **BRIAN DAVIES** who gave his own example, that of the baker and the bread. Where a loaf of bread is tasty, soft and crispy on the outside, we can know that the baker who baked the bread is skilled and proficient. The qualities of the two are different and so when we say 'the bread and the baker are both good' we know that we mean good in different ways. However, we know that the good qualities of the bread are one thing and that good qualities of the baker are another. They are linked but quite different.

C. Analogy of Proportionality

AQUINAS said that all things can be good at their own level. A person is good or bad based on their charity and kindness while a dog is good based on his ability to follow instructions. The expectations are different as each **TELOS** (purpose) is different. **BARON FRIEDERICH VON HÜGEL** said that a dog's faithfulness is not the same as a man's faithfulness. A dog can be good if it does not urinate on your sofa, a husband is good if he does not forget his anniversary. Both are good but to their own degrees. In the same way, when we call a man just it is because he is fair and deals with people in an appropriate way, but to call God just we mean so much more. We know we cannot limit

God to our sense of fairness, and so God may not be fair as we see fairness, but we know that in His infinite way, God must be just. God is infinitely greater than us, yet God is good in his justice and love.

We see this emulated in Ian **RAMSEY's** use of models and qualifiers. We identify the models in this world and through our experiences: goodness, justice, love etc. But we accept that the extent to which they qualify differ dramatically. Our goodness is limited to what humans can possibly do, but God's goodness is infinite and so is immeasurable. But that does not mean that we do not know what are describing.

D. Evaluation

Strengths of the Cataphatic Way

1. **ANALOGY** allows the use of **POSITIVE LANGUAGE** to make meaningful statements about God.

2. **ANALOGY** allows members of religious groups to use religious language to build an understanding of God and build a relationship with God.

3. **ANALOGY** is used by religious believers and exists within revelation and scripture.

4. **ARISTOTLE**: We can see Aristotelian influences in Aquinas' Analogy of Attribution and Proportionality:

   - Analogy of **ATTRIBUTION**: Aristotle described how everything has four causes, and so if the telos of one is a certain way, it reveals something of the nature of the efficient cause.

   - Analogy of **PROPORTIONALITY**: The final cause of each thing is determined by its nature and so can only be good in its own way. God is infinite with a telos well beyond ours. We can use our language without being about to reach the fullness of God's telos.

Weaknesses of the Cataphatic Way

1. William **BLACKSTONE** argued that any **ANALOGY** must always be translated into **UNIVOCAL** language to make any literal sense. This is an echo of David Hume's challenge to the teleological argument - an analogy can only compare two things that are similar: the world is more like a cabbage than a machine.

2. Stephen **EVANS** argued that there was nothing wrong with accepting that knowledge of God is limited. God is a mystery, all we need know is enough so that we can worship him.

3. Rudolph **OTTO** who said that religious language need only show the mysterium tremendum et fascinans (awesome mystery) of God and that we should not worry about trying to say anything literal about God.

5.3 Symbolism

A. What are Signs and Symbols?

SYMBOLS can be linguistic, pictorial or gestural:

- Pictorial symbols may be images of the crucifix or a crescent moon.

- gestural **SYMBOLS** may be kneeling in front of a tabernacle or ritual washing etc.

- Linguistic **SYMBOLS** are no less common, and in fact they appear throughout language.

John **MACQUARRIE** who discusses arbitrary and conventional symbols, where the prior is arbitrarily selected and the latter is involved in an intimate and significant way with the event.

We can see this in religious **SYMBOLS** as a cross is more than an arbitrarily selected picture; it participates in the event of being Christian as Christians are followers of Jesus of Nazareth who was crucified on a cross. Therefore, the wearing of a cross connects the wearer to the event of Jesus' crucifixion naming the wearer as a member of that group of believers and holding all the beliefs they share. However, if a Christian were to become a nun, the wearing of a black and white habit is arbitrary; she could easily wear a blue and red habit.

B. Paul Tillich on Signs and Symbols

- A **SIGN** is arbitrarily chosen to point to something other than itself. There is some debate here as heavy clouds are a sign of rain. The heavy clouds are not arbitrary, but they are also not selected by humans and so we can accept this as an exception to Tillich's point.

- A **SYMBOL** is greater than a sign, not only does it point to something else; it indicates that something special is happening. A candle at a tabernacle symbolises the eternal presence, something is happening and we should take notice.

Paul **TILLICH** argued that religious language is **SYMBOLIC** language in the sense that it communicates significant meanings and understanding about God. He described God as "The Ground of Our Being". This means that God was the basis of all that existed and the reason for all that exists; nothing else was of importance, material possessions and ideas cannot replace God. However, since it is impossible for us to comprehend the ground of our being directly and personally, we do so through **SYMBOLS**. Ideas such as atonement, eternal life and sacrifice and even the life and work of Jesus become **SYMBOLS** to reveal to us this ultimate truth of God. Tillich argued that society is what gives and what can take away the meaning of **SYMBOLS**. However, **SYMBOLS** cannot be destroyed; attempts to destroy **SYMBOLS** in a society often has the opposite effect of it becoming more powerful, e.g. the Christian **ICHTHUS** was used by Christians in the Roman times. Tillich insisted that the greatest strength of a symbol was that it not only indicated a greater event, it **PARTICIPATED** in the event to which it pointed. While non-users may recognise the symbol, e.g. the Ichthus, only users will understand them.

C. The use of Symbols in Scripture and Religious Language

1. Symbols within Scripture

GENESIS: The Creation Stories that appear in Genesis 1 and 2 are taken by most Christian traditions, including the Catholic Church, as being symbolic. This is not to mean they are not 'true', but they contain '**SYMBOLIC** truth'. In Genesis 1, God creates the world in six days. This is **SYMBOLIC** as it gave the Hebrews the seven day week structure against which they built their lives. In Genesis 2, God creates woman from man, this is symbolic to show the intimate dependence of man and woman on each other. In fact, the same chapter cites the belief about marriage and how man and woman become "one flesh".

PSALMS: The Psalms are 'songs of praise' filled with symbolic imagery for God. In the famous Psalm 23, The Lord is called "my Shepherd". This is not to say that we should look at God as a man who stands in a field following sheep around. But as a **SYMBOLIC** phrase, it means that we should depend on God in the way that sheep depend on the shepherd. The symbol calls us to view the words in a different way. They say what we understand to mean what we cannot possibly know first-hand.

2. Symbols within Religious Tradition

LAMB OF GOD: One of Jesus Christ's titles is Lamb of God. In ancient Jewish culture, men and women would sacrifice animals at the Temple in order to atone for their sins. Through the spilling of the blood of the lamb, the sins would be washed away. The penitent would be cleansed by the blood of the sacrifice. When Jesus Christ was crucified on the cross, Christians believe Jesus paid for their sins. In this way, Jesus was the sacrificial lamb whose blood washes away our sins. So we **SYMBOLICALLY** call Jesus the Lamb of God.

ICHTHUS: In Greek, the word for fish is ichthus. This word is an acronym for the Greek words: Iesous, Christos, Theou, (h)yios and soter, in English: Jesus

Christ, Son of God and Saviour. In early Christian times when Christians were persecuted, it was not safe to announce one's religion, and so drawing the simply image of a fish was a symbol that one believed in Jesus Christ, Son of God and Saviour, identifying them as a Christian to whoever understood that symbol, but protecting them against anyone who did not.

D. Evaluation

Strengths of Symbolism

1. **TRANSCENDENT**: Symbols go beyond language and culture. If pictorial or gestural, they do not need language at all. If they are linguistic, they last beyond the language themselves.

2. **NON-LITERAL**: Symbols convey ideas about God that cannot be literally expressed. They give rise to analogical beliefs, using language believers can grasp.

3. **PARTICIPATION**: Symbols participate in what they are referring and so several ideas and notions can be carried by a simple word or phrase.

Weaknesses of Symbolism

1. **CHANGING**: Symbols can be bastardised into something else, e.g. the Swastika. This means that they are not pure in their use.

2. **REDUCTION**: Symbols can have various meanings and are often the product of a time and place. Therefore, their original meaning may be lost and their value may be reduced. The **SYMBOL** of God as a shepherd does not have the same value in 21st Century England as it did in 1st Century BC in Israel where it emerged.

3. **EPISTEMIC DISTANCE**: Symbols are human creations and still do not bridge the epistemic distance (knowledge gap) between God and man.

Confusions to Avoid

1. A question on religious language is not asking you whether or not God exists or to prove that God exists. Rather it is asking you about the **LANGUAGE** we use to discuss God in the first place. Avoid picking weaknesses in the different forms of language on the basis that they cannot "prove" God or because you think there is no God. This is not the question. Keep on track.

2. A question on Classical Religious Language may either ask for an analysis of one particular type of religious language or be open and ask for comparisons between different types of religious language. In both cases, students are expected to analyse the named form of religious language and make comparisons with other forms of religious language. However, it is very important to note that students are not supposed to write three separate essays. The primary focus should be on the **FORM OF LANGUAGE** specified in the question, and then comparisons should be drawn with the other forms of religious language.

3. For example, if the question is about **ANALOGY**, students should fully analyse **ANALOGY** with its strengths and weaknesses, and then compare it against **VIA NEGATIVA**, showing how **VIA NEGATIVA** resolves the problem that **ANALOGY** has in anthropomorphising God. Conversely, show how Aquinas moved away from **VIA NEGATIVA** as religious language means more than negation. The comparisons should be direct. It is a common and avoidable error to write about one type of religious language and then in the next paragraph write about another form disconnected from the previous paragraphs showing no connection between the paragraphs and with no link back to the question.

Key Quotes

"I do not merely declare that he who affirms attributes of God has not sufficient knowledge concerning the Creator ... but I say that he unconsciously loses his belief in God." – Moses Maimonides

"In regard to what they express, these words apply literally to God... But as regards their manner of expressing it, they don't apply literally to God; for their manner of expression is appropriate only to creatures." – St Thomas Aquinas

"When we say "God is alive" we mean more than "God is not mortally dead". – St Thomas Aquinas

"I went at once to my confessor, to tell him about it. He asked me in what form I had seen Him. I told him that I had not seen Him at all." – Teresa of Avila

"The Conventional symbol has no connection with what it symbolises... The intrinsic symbol, on the other hand, has in itself a kinship with what it symbolises." – John MacQuarrie

"God] is beyond assertion since he is 'the perfect and unique cause of all things'. He is beyond denial by virtue of his 'pre-eminently simple and absolute nature, free from every limitation, beyond every limitation." – Pseudo-Dionysius

Suggested Reading

Moses Maimonides, A Guide to the Perplexed, Chapter LX

Paul Tillich, Dynamics of Faith, Chapters 3-4

John MacQuarrie, Principles of Christian Theology, Chapter 24 The Modes of Theological Discourse

Practise Exam Question

'The best approach to understanding religious language is through the Cataphatic Way.' Discuss.

AO1 Demonstrate knowledge and understanding through the use of some of the following material. (Maximum 16 marks)

- Outline the meaning of 'Cataphatic Way'.

- Present Aquinas' two forms of analogy: Attribution and Proportionality.

- Give examples for each including Brian Davies' example and Von Hugel's dog example.

AO2 Demonstrate evaluation and analysis through the use of some of the following arguments (maximum 24 marks)

- Identify the weaknesses with using a Cataphatic approach, including Blackstone and Hume's challenge on analogy.

- Explore the similarities between Analogy and Symbolism and the differences.

- Explore Aquinas' rejection of the Apophatic Way and why he preferred the Cataphatic Way.

- Explore the successes of analogy over Via Negativa and Symbolism, e.g. giving believers a platform to discuss God.

- Explore how they are more superior in other ways, e.g. illustrating the epistemic distance of man from God etc.

- Compare Analogy against the other forms of religious language and draw a conclusion.

Possible Future Questions

1. To what extent is the Via Negativa the only way to talk about God?

2. Evaluate the claim that analogy can successfully be used to express the human understanding of God.

3. Critically assess the views of Paul Tillich on religious language.

6. Twentieth Century Perspectives on Religious Language

Key Terms

BLIK – A statement made from a personal or shared paradigm where only the claimant can decides what is evidence against the assertion.

FALSIFICATION – The truth or falseness of a statement can be tested by empirical observation.

GOD-TALK – Any statements made pertaining to the existence of God.

LANGUAGE GAME – The belief that language only makes sense within a given context.

LOGICAL POSITIVISM – The belief in Verificationism.

VERIFICATION – Proving something to be true.

Specification

		A. The Principle of Verification
6. Twentieth Century Perspectives on Religious Language	6.1 Logical Positivism	A. The Principle of Verification B. Ayer's Variations of the Principle of Verification
	6.2 Language Games	A. Wittgenstein's Language Games B. Evaluation
	6.3 Falsification Symposium	A. Falsification B. Bliks C. Falsification Parables

6.1 Logical Positivism

A. The Principle of Verification

The 18th Century thinker David **HUME** argued that there were two areas of human study:

- **RELATIONS OF IDEAS** – analytic statements which are rationally known

- **MATTERS OF FACT** – synthetic statements which are empirically shown

We see this idea reflected in the 1920's **LOGICAL POSITIVIST** movement of the Vienna Circle, chaired by Moritz Schlick, which postulated that the only statements that have factual meaning are those which can be sense observed or **TAUTOLOGIES**. Loosely this means synthetic and analytic statements. The implication of this is that all statements which are not synthetic or analytic are deemed to be factually meaningless. This includes statements of art, morality and more intentionally religion and any form of **GOD-TALK**. This accidentally ended up including statements of history and many statements of science.

The statement finds an immediate problem in its own formation: The only meaningful statements are sense observable or tautologies. The statement itself is neither a sense observable nor is it a tautology. Additionally, Richard **SWINBURNE** pointed out that very few statements, even within the world of science, could be sense observed. For example, to state 'water boils at 100 degrees Celsius' would require all water in the universe to be boiled, and the statement 'humans are mortal' could never be meaningful as it would require all humans to be killed and then no one would be alive to state it. Swinburne used Carl **HEMPLE**'s classic example of stating 'Ravens are black'; without observing every raven one cannot declare that statement **VERIFIED**.

B. Ayer's Variations of the Principle of Verification

A. J. **AYER** took it upon himself in Language, Truth and Logic to adapt and make sense of the Principle of **VERIFICATION**, however, he found himself constantly barraged by challenges, which show the principle largely unsustainable.

i. Version 1, Modification 1: Strong and Weak Verification

Strong **VERIFICATION** - stating something using sense observation here and now. There is clear evidence for it and it can be state conclusively.

Weak **VERIFICATION** - statements confirmed though **INDUCTIVE** reasoning. It is probably the case based on past evidence and verification. We do not need to observe it in the strong sense, but if new observations change our ideas then they are taken on board. We find that most scientific knowledge is weakly verified, e.g. that water boils at 100 degrees, that humans are mortal etc.

This form of **VERIFICATION** still found criticism and challenge. Richard Swinburne argued that there are plenty of things that cannot be **VERIFIED** even weakly that are meaningful to discuss, e.g. history, theoretical physics and quantum physics etc. These cannot be verified even weakly and yet we discuss them as though they have meaning.

ii. Version 1, Modification 2: Verification in Practice and Principle

VERIFICATION IN PRACTICE is like strong verification where it can be verified in the here and now and can be seen as conclusive.

VERIFICATION IN PRINCIPLE is the verification where we accept the limitation of what we can practically verify, however, since we know how we would verify something that cannot be weakly verified, we are able to discuss it. For example, even though I cannot see a quark or quantum strings I know the theory of how I would be able to verify them and so it is meaningful to discuss it. Furthermore, even though we have no proof of aliens, we know how we would verify them, by visiting all planets etc. Even though it is not practical, it is in principle possible and so it is verifiable.

However, this led to **HICK**'s challenge. God is verifiable in principle. He gave the Parable of the **CELESTIAL CITY** where two travellers are walking on a road. One is convinced that there is a celestial city at the end of the road and the other is not. The first argues that eventually they will either arrive at a city or not, at which point they will be able to verify or **FALSIFY** the city's existence. In the same way, eschatologically we will be able to verify or **FALSIFY** God's existence. Additionally, I know how I would prove God's existence, with a miracle or a vision etc. Therefore, **GOD-TALK** is meaningful as God can be verified.

Incidentally, a good response to Hick is that **ESCHATOLOGICALLY** one cannot 'verify' anything as one is dead without the senses to verify anything.

iii. Version 2: Direct and Indirect Verification

DIRECT VERIFICATION considers meaningful any statement that is *"itself an observation-statement, or is such that in conjunction with one or more observation-statements it entails at least one observation-statement." (Ayer)*. The example Ayer gave was that of Torricelli's endeavour to prove the changes in atmospheric pressure by taking a barometer to the top of a mountain and directly verifying that mercury rose.

INDIRECT VERIFICATION considers meaningful any statement that, while not being directly verifiable, *"in conjunction with certain other premises it entails one or more directly verifiable statements which are not deducible from these other premises alone." (Ayer)*. Ayer's example was that of **GALILEO**, who proved the changes in atmospheric pressure indirectly by dropping two objects of different weights at a height and showing they landed at the same time. While this did not prove atmospheric pressure directly, it was evidence that reveals it indirectly. The focus here is on evidence. If there is evidence for something, you do not need to verify it directly. There is evidence to suggest it, so it is meaningful to discuss it.

Ultimately, however, the fact that statements about history and art cannot be verified even indirectly showed the ultimate limitations of **LOGICAL POSITIVISM** and the theory was eventually abandoned.

6.2 Wittgenstein's Language Games

A. Language as a Form of Life

Ludwig **WITTGENSTEIN** began his career as a **LOGICAL POSITIVIST** writing in his Tractatus *"whereof one cannot speak, thereof one must remain silent"*, but then changed his way of thinking by the time he wrote his Philosophical Investigations having revised his entire approach to philosophy.

Wittgenstein argued that language is not a rigid set of terms or formulae, but rather it adapts and grows. He called it a **LEBENSFORM**, a **FORM OF LIFE**. It is unique to the people engaging in the language and is meaningful to them. He developed a theory that language was ever growing and adapting and it only makes sense in very specific contexts and as such could not be subject to verification. He gave the example of builders working on a site where they use terms such as 'plank' and 'block'. When the foreman calls the term the workers know what he wants and brings it to him. This dialogue, Wittgenstein argued, was an example of a primitive language, which is unique to builders.

Normal **MALCOLM** supported the view of language as lebensform. He argued that all language is contextual and only makes sense in their proper contexts. He further commented that atheists see religious language as an *"alien form of life"*; hence, they do not understand how to engage with it.

LANGUAGE GAMES directly responds to and undermines the challenges of **LOGICAL POSITIVISM**. Logical Positivist notions that meaningful statements must be **VERIFIABLE** make perfect sense within the context and language game of science and maths, but not in the language game of **GOD-TALK**. Therefore, Language Games liberates God-Talk and allows that it belongs within the Language Game of theology and religious belief.

All forms of language, **GOD-TALK**, morality, history, art, music etc. are language games of their own. We all speak multiple language games depending on where we are and what we are doing. We adapt our language to our audiences and one use of language, e.g. Italian, sport, Star Wars terminology, would have no meaning in another, e.g. on a driving test you would not say "the Force is with you", and in an English exam you would not write in Italian. Language is always **CONTEXTUAL**.

B. Meaningful not Cognitive

In the same way that chess has its own language and uses of terms, so does football and the two are distinct, therefore, to be 'check mated' is meaningless in football, as much as being 'off-side' means nothing in chess. The terms make sense in their contexts but **OBJECTIVELY** they have no meaning.

Wittgenstein called the business of using language in its context a **LANGUAGE GAME**. He argued that the use of language was not private but public within a community, and each language using community is different, e.g. the community of English speakers, the community of chess players, the community of mathematicians. Language can only make sense when it is used with other members of that language using community. In the community of theism, statements such as "God is good" make sense, but statements like "F=MA" mean nothing. The implication of this is that while it has contextual meaning, language itself has no objective meaning, it is **NON-COGNITIVE**.

In separating different types of talk as different language games Wittgenstein removed the link between **GOD-TALK** and objective truth. Thus, God-Talk is both redeemed by calling it a different language game, so atheists can no longer call it meaningless, and also punished, as it suggests that you cannot make an objective empirical or historical statements about religious ideas as they only have meaning in a "religious context".

This is a problem for believers who do not think that their God-Talk is nothing more than a secret language that they use to help understand each other. Religious believers are convinced that their language conveys truths about the objective universe. Language games does not allow this to be the case. It compartmentalises all language into its own game. While there are crossovers, e.g. mathematical formulae (**MATHS-TALK**) being used in physics (**SCIENCE-TALK**) and discussion of Jesus Christ (**CHRISTIANITY-TALK**) coming from Nazareth (**GEOGRAPHY-TALK**), there is no cognitive truth to any language. Language itself is made up.

Ultimately, Wittgenstein was arguing that God-Talk is meaningful to participants in the **GOD-TALK LANGUAGE GAME**, but not to anyone not participating in the game.

6.3 Falsification Symposium

A. Falsification

i. Flew's Falsification

Anthony **FLEW** argued that **GOD-TALK** was meaningless because it was **UNFALSIFIABLE**. By this, he meant that believers make their claims about God but do not accept any basis by which their claims might be refuted. By not accepting such refutations, believers make their claims **UNFALSIFIABLE** and so meaningless.

Flew argued that when we make assertions we unconsciously refute the negation of that assertion, so if I assert 'my pen is black' I am unconsciously asserting 'my pen is not red, blue, green or any other colour than black'. This way, I am allowing that if it could be shown that my pen is green, it would refute my original assertion. If we do not allow any conditions for the negation, then we are unconsciously omitting any conditions for the assertion itself. If I do not allow that my pen is categorically NOT green, then should my pen be revealed to be green, I might deny that my original assertion was false by modifying it to say: 'my pen is black, or green.' Thus my original assertion means nothing.

Flew used John **WISDOM**'s Parable of the **EXPLORERS** (and the Gardener) to emphasise his point; when two explorers happen on a garden in a forest, one asserts "there is a gardener", but the second shows all evidence to the contrary. However, no evidence will shake the first's resolve and he maintains "there is an intangible, invisible, inaudible gardener". The second declares: "what remains of your original assertion?" **FLEW** maintained that when believers are faced with evidence that contradicts their assertions, like "God loves me", or "God has a plan", they are so vague and void of any refutations of negations, that the assertion "dies a death of a thousand qualifications" and becomes "factually meaningless".

ii. Popper's Falsification

THE PRINCIPLE OF FALSIFICATION is first brought to light by Karl **POPPER** in Conjectures and Refutations where he is responding to what he called pseudo-science, that is astrology and Freudian psychology. He argued that such disciplines masquerade as science but are themselves not actual science as they fail the test of falsification and have no actual scientific basis.

He argued that if any claim was to be considered **SCIENTIFIC**, it must be in principle falsifiable. For example, if one were to claim 'water boils at 100 degrees Celsius', they are claiming that it does not boil at 98, 99, 101, 102 etc. Should it be shown that water boils at 101 degrees Celsius, then it shows the original assertion false, but still scientific as it was subject to falsification. Science is the process of attempting to disprove assertions. If an assertion has no principle basis for falsification, then it is not scientific. For example: 'your fortune will grow as Mars moves into Pisces' or 'men want to kill their fathers and marry their mothers'. Such assertions are not scientific as there is no principle basis for falsification. Popper called this the principle of demarcation between what is science and what is pseudo-science.

FLEW takes this principle and assumes that it demarcates between what is meaningful and meaningless. But this is *not* present in Popper's original thesis. To assume that falsificationism can demarcate between meaningful and meaningless language is to change Popper's original thesis. This is what Flew appears to do. For Flew if a statement is not *falsifiable*, then, not only is it not scientific, but it is not meaningful either.

B. Bliks

R. M. **HARE** responded to Flew's challenge of **FALSIFICATION** by presenting the notion of **BLIKS**, claims that may well be unfalsifiable but are nonetheless meaningful to us as they influence the way we see the world and live our lives. Hare presented the parable of the lunatic student who is convinced that his dons (tutors) are out to kill him. Despite how many mild-mannered dons are presented to him by his friends, he maintains that it is a rouse and that they want him dead. Hare admits that the student is a lunatic and that his assertion is indeed unfalsifiable. However, he maintains that it is still meaningful to him. It affects his life, and he alone can control what counts as evidence.

Hare discussed what people really believe and think about things. He gives his own example of being utterly convinced that the steering column in his car works. If he did not believe it, he would not drive. His blik that the steering column works affects his life as he drives his car. Were he to have any **REASON** to believe that it did not work, he would not drive. Hare argues that we all have bliks about everything whether or not we have thought about it and we alone are in control of what counts as evidence for or against it. Just as the friends of the student are convinced by the dons' mild-manner, the lunatic is not and he alone controls the evidence that may convince him one day.

What we really believe is what forms our bliks. Bliks determine what **EVIDENCE** you accept. They are shared and life changing. For Hare, religious language is meaningful as it is about what people **BELIEVE**. In this way, Flew's falsification does not threaten religious language because unfalsifiable statements can still hold meaning for users and can still be bliks.

C. Falsification Parables

A number of other philosophers participated in the Falsification Symposium and presented their own parables to help explain religious language:

- **PARABLE OF THE EXPLORERS**: John **WISDOM**, who originally wrote the Parable of the Explorers (and the gardener) as a dialectic about the way different people see evidence for God, argued that God cannot be **VERIFIED** or **FALSIFIED** as He is not part of what we traditionally consider scientific.

- **PARABLE OF THE PARTISAN AND THE STRANGER**: Basil **MITCHELL** wrote the parable of the Partisan in a country occupied by an enemy nation. He meets a stranger who impresses him greatly and is convinced that the stranger is an ally. When the stranger is seen helping friends the partisan declares "see, he is on our side", and when he is seen helping the enemy, the partisan declares "he must have a reason to behave that way". This is a reflection of how believers **INTERPRET** good and bad events as though God is still good.

Mitchell warned that believers should not allow religious beliefs to be vacuous formulae, but that experience should in fact make a difference. For example, if I believe "Thor makes the lightning", what of all the evidence that shows that lightning is a natural phenomenon? Will I deny the evidence to maintain my **BLIND FAITH**? Mitchell argues that we should not do that. In this way, falsification does help to demarcate between what is meaningful and what is meaningless, though not to the extent that Flew does.

- **TOYS IN THE CUPBOARD**: Richard Swinburne present the idea that we can talk meaningfully about toys in a cupboard that come alive when no-one is watching. While this is not falsifiable, it does not change that it is still meaningful to discuss it. It may be **UNSCIENTIFIC**, but it is not **MEANINGLESS**.

Confusions to Avoid

1. The questions are referring to the meaningfulness and meaninglessness of talking about God, not the existence of God. It would be a mistake to assume that **AYER** and **SCHLICK** are making direct assaults on the existence of God. That said, it could be argued that their attacks on **GOD-TALK** are camouflaged attacks on religion as without language one cannot have a functioning religion. If the language is declared meaningless, then the tenets of faith have no basis.

2. Students may want to refer to George **ORWELL**'s 1984 where Newspeak is created with the sole purpose of diminishing the scope of human thinking in order to control the populace. There is reason to hold this view considering the extent that Ayer went to modify the principle of verification to allow for science-talk, history-talk but not God-talk or ethics.

3. **FALSIFICATIONISM** is not primarily a discussion on meaningfulness and meaninglessness of religious language. There is a divide as to whether it can be used at all in a question on whether or not **GOD-TALK** is meaningful. When asked, this question does refer to **VERIFICATIONISM**; however, the reality is that Anthony Flew specifically stated: *"Believers will allow nothing to falsify their belief claims. Therefore, God-Talk is meaningless as it is unfalsifiable."* So it is clear that he considered religious language to be meaningless on the basis of **FALSIFICATION**. However, students should be wary that this may not be what the examiner wants to see.

If **FALSIFICATION** is going to be used on a question about meaningfulness, it should be done with care, referring to Flew's quote and Popper's original use of the principle of demarcation.

Key Quotes

"Falsification is demarcating scientific statements from other kinds of statements." – Karl Popper

"If relentlessly pursued, the theologian will have to resort to avoiding action of qualification. And there lies that death by a thousand qualifications, which would, I agree, constitute a failure in faith as well as in logic." – Anthony Flew

"Believers will allow nothing to falsify their belief claims. Therefore, God-Talk is meaningless as it is unfalsifiable." – Anthony Flew

"The nature of God is totally outside of our traditional methods of scientific enquiry – as a result is God-Talk meaningless?" – John Wisdom

"At the end of the day, if God does exist, then the verification of his existence is verifiable in principle, but if God does not exist, then his existence is not falsifiable." – John Hick

"A Blik is a claim about the world that is not falsifiable nor can it be tested." – R. M. Hare

"The obsessive concern with the proofs of the existence of God reveals the assumption that in order for religious belief to be intellectually respectable it ought to have a rational justification. That is the misunderstanding. It is like the idea that we are not justified in relying on memory until memory has been proved reliable..."
– Normal Malcolm

"Theists do not accept evidence that counts against their beliefs Believers have to take care that religious beliefs are not just 'vacuous formulae to which experience makes no difference and which makes no difference to life." – Basil Mitchell

Suggested Reading

A. J. Ayer, Language, Truth and Logic, Chapter 1 The Elimination of Metaphysics

Antony Flew, Theology and Falsification, excerpt published in Reason and Responsibility 1968

R.M. Hare, A Map of Twentieth Century Philosophy, Chapter 11 Theology and Language, section 28

Karl Popper, Conjectures and Refutations, Chapter 11 The Demarcation between Science and Metaphysics

Ludwig Wittgenstein, Philosophical Investigations, 2. 7. 23. 31.

Practise Exam Question

How successful does the language games concept make sense of religious language?

AO1 Demonstrate knowledge and understanding through the use of some of the following material. (Maximum 16 marks)

- Outline what Wittgenstein said about language being a lebensform.

- Explain how Language Games operate. Use examples, e.g. the builder, chess and football.

- Briefly outline the challenge the Logical Positivism makes for God-talk.

- Explain how Language Games makes sense of religious language in response to the challenges made by Logical Positivism.

AO2 Demonstrate evaluation and analysis through the use of some of the following arguments (maximum 24 marks)

- Explain how Language Games makes language meaningful and yet non-cognitive.

- Explain why religious people might reject Wittgenstein's Language Games on the basis that it removes objective meaning from religious statements.

- Explore Normal Malcolm's view that Language is contextual. Show how that supports Language Games.

- Compare the strengths of Language Games with its weaknesses and draw a conclusion.

Possible Future Questions

1. Critically assess Wittgenstein's belief that language games allow religious statements to have meaning.

2. The falsification principle presents no real challenge to religious belief. Discuss

3. Critically assess the claim that religious language is meaningless.

Exam Rescue Remedy

Introductions should include:

1. **Definition of terms**: Identification of the theories/arguments referred to the title.

2. **Identification of the parameters of the question**: what are

the two opposing perspectives?

3. **Thesis statement**: Where do you stand in the argument?

You should plan six paragraphs including:

1. **Title**: Discuss the arguments referred to in the title.

2. **Challenge 1**: Discuss the weaknesses or against the arguments of paragraph 1.

3. **Response 1**: Respond to the weaknesses and challenges discussed in paragraph 2. Summarise or omit if the thesis statement agrees with paragraph 1.

4. **Alternative**: Discuss an alternative/opposing perspective to the arguments of paragraph 1.

5. **Challenge 2**: Discuss the weaknesses or against the arguments of paragraph 4.

6. **Response 2**: Respond to the weaknesses and challenges discussed in paragraph 5. Summarise or omit if the thesis statement disagrees with paragraph 1.

Each paragraph should include:

1. **Hook**: What will this paragraph be about? What scholar/work? Why is this relevant?

2. **Assertions**: What are the attitudes/beliefs/teachings that the scholars present?

3. **Analysis**: How do these assertions work? Why are they presented? How do they form an argument?

4. **Justification**: What examples/quotes defend and justify the assertions made?

5. **Link**: How does this paragraph answer the question? How does it link

to your thesis statement?

Conclusions should include:

1. **For**: Summarise the arguments for one side of the question.

2. **Against**: Summarise the arguments for the alternative side of the question.

3. **Evaluation**: Evaluate the perspectives and justify the thesis statement.

Postscript

Andrew Capone is the Head of RE at St Simon Stock Catholic School, Maidstone. He has a Masters of Arts in Classical History and a Joint Bachelors of Arts in Philosophy and Religious Studies. He also offers personal tuition, analytical marking and consultation to RE and Philosophy teachers.

He is always willing to discuss and share work and resources, and support both students and teachers of the subject. Philosophy is a subject shared.

www.peped.org

Printed in Great Britain
by Amazon